Let Me Tell You ...

People Of Faith
Speak To Their Times
And Ours

David G. Rogne

CSS Publishing Company, Inc., Lima, Ohio

LET ME TELL YOU ...

Scripture quotations marked (NRSV) are from the *New Revised Standard Version of the
Bible*, copyright 1989 by the Division of Christian Education of the National Council of
the Churches of Christ in the USA. Used by permission.

Scripture quotations marked (RSV) are from the *Revised Standard Version of the Bible*,
copyrighted 1946, 1952 ©, 1971, 1973, by the Division of Christian Education of the
National Council of the Churches of Christ in the USA. Used by permission.

Library of Congress Cataloging-in-Publication Data

Rogne, David George, 1934-
    Let me tell you : people of faith speak to their times and ours / David G. Rogne.
        p.   cm.
    ISBN 0-7880-1869-8 (alk. paper)
    1. Bible—Biography—Meditations. I. Title
BS571 .R65 2001
270'.092'2—dc21   2001037936
                                                                          CIP

For more information about CSS Publishing Company resources, visit our website at
www.csspub.com.

ISBN 0-7880-1869-8   PRINTED IN U.S.A.

*For Maureen and Lisa
Two PKs Who Made
Life In The Parsonage Interesting*

Table Of Contents

Introduction

One of the ways in which people of faith are helped to address their current situations with courage and strength is by becoming aware of the legacy of experience and encouragement passed on by those who have traveled the path of faithfulness and duty before them. The circumstances of those who have gone before may have been different from ours, but the call to service and faithfulness is a constant, which makes their lives relevant to ours.

One problem we all have in availing ourselves of the strength that could come from the faithful responses of others is our own ignorance of those people and their faith journeys. In the chapters which follow, I have attempted to present salient features of the lives of twelve persons of faith in relatively brief monologues. The monologues by no means exhaust the possible messages we could receive from the persons chosen. However, it is my hope that the characteristics highlighted present possible attitudes of the characters as they faced their own circumstances and as they share observations that may be pertinent to our time as well.

We may wonder what a sheik wandering the desert some 4,000 years ago could have to say to our age. But Abraham was a wanderer, cut off from his roots in the same way many corporate gypsies today are destined to move from opportunity to opportunity without a settled home. Abraham may have some advice for them.

Is there such a thing as Divine Providence operative in our lives? Does God have any involvement in the way things work out? Those who recorded the story of Joseph in the book of Genesis certainly felt that God is active in human life. They quote Joseph as saying that God can bring good out of human evil intentions. This may be a helpful word to those who feel that they are going through dark times through no fault of their own.

Can people of average talents and gifts make a difference? Most of us are in that category, and we would really like to know. The attributes of Moses God found most useful were those that in themselves were quite ordinary. The message of Moses is that each of us has unique gifts that we can use in forwarding God's purposes.

Human nature tends to identify national interests with God's interests. The people of Jeremiah's time felt that God was uniquely their God. As Jeremiah lived through the events of his time he came to the conclusion that true religion is neither national nor institutional, but personal. He warns us that we do not bend God to our will, but rather, that we must submit ourselves to God's will.

Jesus' ministry had a social action dimension from the beginning. The writer of the Gospel of Luke records words attributed to Jesus' mother, Mary, which appear to be modeled on the words of Hannah in 1 Samuel. Zechariah, a kinsman of Mary, tells us how this came about, and at the same time prepares subsequent followers of Jesus to expect a revolutionary message.

It has never been easy to stand in the shadow of another who is thought to be an equal. Andrew stood in the shadow of his brother, Peter, and he learned some lessons that help us to see that every one of us has something to offer in service to God.

Most of us have had experiences that cause us to doubt God's involvement in life. Thomas, one of the disciples of Jesus, was no exception, but his life demonstrates that one can move beyond doubt and become a useful disciple.

Some persons mistakenly believe that the reward for faithful discipleship is protection from hardship and suffering. As the Apostle Paul relates his story, it is evident that is not the case. Nevertheless, faithful discipleship does produce courage and provide one with satisfaction.

"No one has greater love than this, to lay down one's life for one's friends," said Jesus. That is as true in our day as when Jesus uttered it. Father Damien, working among the lepers of Molokai, shows us how far love may ask us to go.

To a generation that hardly understands what it means to be guided by one's principles, Eric Liddell presents an interesting challenge. While the people of our generation may not be disturbed by what troubled him, the fact that a person would give up an opportunity for fame because of a principle catches our interest. As

Liddell tells of his life subsequent to the 1924 Olympics, it becomes evident that God honored Liddell's choices with even greater challenges.

How far should a Christian go in resisting evil? Dietrich Bonhoeffer faced that question and decided the issue in a way that may help others who are dealing with the question. Among the many lessons we learn from his life, we learn that each of us is called to live our life for others.

Do Christians still have a responsibility to go and make disciples of all nations? It may help those of us who do little to spread the gospel to be exposed to the lives of others, like Jim Elliot, who are prepared to give their lives to tell others about the love of God.

It is the author's hope that these monologues will provide examples of how God is and has been at work in the lives of countless people of faith to provide guidance, encouragement, and hope.

1. Father Of The Faithful

Genesis 12-25

A name can be a difficult thing to live up to. When I was born my parents named me "Abram," which, in our language, means "Exalted Father." But my name was to become even more demanding, for some things happened in my life which led to my name being changed to "Abraham," which means "Father of a Multitude." I did indeed become father of the nation of Israel, a people who eventually came to live in all the lands of the world. There are those people who say that I am also the father, in a spiritual sense, of all who put their trust in God. I don't want to go that far, but I do want to tell you of certain developments in my life which made my life happy and fruitful, because I think that those experiences might help some of you to find the fulfilling life we are all seeking.

The first significant development in my life had to do with my relationship to God. Like many people, I would have to acknowledge that my early training was religious. I was born in the ancient seaport city of Ur, where the Euphrates River pours into the Persian Gulf — a land which today would be called Iraq. My father and brothers were moon-worshipers, and to a degree, so was I. In fact, my father was so devoted to this cult that he moved our whole family to a center of moon worship in Assyria. There we stayed, following the religious customs of my family, as long as my father lived. But within me there was a growing dissatisfaction with this approach to religion. It was as though a small voice was telling me that God was not to be found through these carefully rehearsed rituals of my family.

Then, when my father died and I became head of the clan, that small voice within me grew louder. It seemed to be calling me away from my present environment and way of life and telling me to move west into a land that I did not know. I thought about it for a long time. Reason would dictate that I stay where things were comfortable, where I was acquainted, where I had security. But that inner voice kept saying, "Trust me. Trust me."

Therefore, in an act of complete trust in the providence of the God who was calling me, I left behind the security of the old ways and embarked on a journey that can best be described as a journey of faith. I brought all of my family and my flocks and herds together and set out for a land to which I felt God would bring me.

I am not seeking to promote foolhardiness or suggesting that everyone here should go home, pack his things, and move to some other place. What I *am* suggesting, from my own experience, is that one listen for the inner voice of God that speaks to each one of us. One part of our natures tells us to seek security, to keep things just the way they are, to trust in what we've got. Another part of our natures tells us that changes have to be made in ourselves, in our attitudes, in our style of life, if we are going to find the happiness we seek. It has been my experience that the call for a change is far more likely to be the voice of God than is the call for the status quo. We are far more apt to find the reality of God in the crisis of insecurity than in the comfort of things as they are.

That, I think, is the leap of faith some people talk about. Faith is not a list of propositions that one believes about God. It is not the statement, "I believe that there is a God." Faith is trust. It is entrusting oneself to the care and keeping of God, come what may. It is committing oneself to a way of life, even when you can't see everything revealed clearly before you. It is taking one step at a time in bold confidence that the world is a good place and that the God who is in control of it is fair and just and loving, no matter how people may act. I didn't discover all this at once. It came as a result of taking one step at a time. You don't get anywhere in religious development until you take the step of faith and commit as much of yourself as you can to as much of God as you understand.

A second significant aspect of my life had to do with my relationship to the places where God is worshiped. In my day people said, "You don't have to be attached to a particular place to worship God." I suppose that some are still saying that. There is sufficient truth in it to make it plausible. Certainly, one's personal faith in God is not the same as one's membership in a particular congregation. Faith is a personal relationship to God that is available to everyone, everywhere — and unless one has some kind of a personal faith, congregational worship is just going through empty motions.

But, in a very real sense, vital religion must be social. If religion is healthy, it must be directed outward in service toward others. If it is valuable, it should lead one to share it with others. If it is growing, it will be strengthened by the experience of others. Solitary religion has neither much joy nor much power. Worshiping together adds a dimension to our religious development which we could not discover alone.

This became very real to me in my moving about. When I settled down in a particular community, if there was a place of worship there, I attached myself to it. If there was no place of worship, I got in and helped build one — I did that at Shechem, at Bethel, and at Hebron. If people want to keep their faith alive, their religious experience vital, I think they need to be related to the worshiping community where they live. Surely that observation applies in your day as well as in mine. I suppose that people still move around as much in your day, as they did in mine. They still need friends; they still need the companionship of like-minded people; they still need channels through which they can serve other people; they still need the challenges to better living which worshiping together can provide.

And yet, how easy it is to drop away. Sometimes when we move, we find that we have so many things to take care of — getting acquainted with the new place, getting our house in order, having guests in — that we really never do get back to the worshiping community. We may have been active where we came from, but the pattern is broken, we get out of the habit, and there are always plenty of other things to take up our time. God doesn't strike us dead for this — there is no immediate deterioration in our religious convictions — but over the long haul our lifestyle changes little by little, our aspirations become more and more materialistic, and God's will becomes less and less relevant. I can only speak for myself — but I confidently feel that an important factor in my religious development was the opportunity to express my faith by identifying with local places of worship.

A third aspect of my religious development had to do with my relationship to material goods. As a sheik, chief of a clan, I had become used to having all that I wanted of everything. I would choose first, then others in the clan would get what was left. But as I learned to rely on God, I found it increasingly easy to be generous. One case in point was the problem of pasture land. My flocks and herds and those of my nephew Lot kept running into each other and competing for the same pasturage. I had the right to claim it for myself and send him elsewhere, but instead, I gave him the right to choose first. He chose the grassy plains, and I was obliged to take to the rocky foothills. But I discovered that I could survive. I didn't have to have the best of everything to get along. God gave me a heart to be content with what was given me.

On another occasion, when I rescued my nephew Lot from a band of marauding soldiers, I came into possession of a great deal of booty which those soldiers had taken from the people of Sodom, where Lot had been living. When the king of Sodom showed up, he asked if he could just have his people back. I told him he could have everything back — people, animals, gold, jewelry — everything. I had a right to keep it, but the prospect of profiting from someone else's grief was repellent to me. I didn't want to be a war profiteer.

Perhaps the most significant change in my attitude was demonstrated when I met Melchizedek, king of Salem, who, in addition to being a king, was also a priest of the God I worshiped. I was so overjoyed to find someone else engaged in the propagation of the faith that I wanted to share in his work. So I tithed all that I had for that purpose. I gave ten percent of everything that I had to help carry on the faith.

I suppose that what I am trying to get across is that when we really trust in God, it affects the way we handle material things. If God really is the Lord of the universe, then everything is ultimately God's. If God gives us certain privileges and wealth, the best we can say for ourselves is that we are temporary trustees. If we really trust God, then we don't have to be so concerned about getting every last thing that is coming to us; we don't have to be stingy in order to protect ourselves; we don't have to be afraid of being generous. Generosity is a product of a healthy relationship with God.

Moreover, attachment to a local congregation of worshiping people gives us a channel through which we can give to the needs of others. A congregation exists to be of service: to bring people to God, to teach faith, to comfort those who are afflicted, to minister to those who are distressed. If a congregation is going to do those things, it needs the generous support of those who are a part of it.

What is the next step for *you* in *your* religious development? Is it to take the first step and commit your way to God? Is it to become a part of a local congregation where you can express that commitment? Or, having accomplished those things, is it to get serious about how you are going to use what God has entrusted to you? These were the steps in my spiritual pilgrimage — as I changed from Abram to Abraham. Perhaps God is speaking to you in a similar way, to lead you from what you *are* to what you are *yet* to be. I urge you to listen to what God is saying to you — and do not be afraid to step out in faith.

2. The Dreamer

Genesis 50:20

My name is Joseph, "Overseer of the Granaries of Upper and Lower Egypt, Royal Seal-Bearer, by reason of wisdom, Father of the King of Egypt, Great Steward of the Lord of the Two Lands, Foremost of Courtiers, Chief of the Entire Land." Such are my titles and such people now call me when they seek my attention. Yet, such noble-sounding titles have not always been my lot, for I was not born noble, neither was I born Egyptian. In fact, it is in humility that I now bear these titles, for I understand that they were conferred by Almighty God.

I do not for one minute think that you are interested in hearing my success story because of who I am. But perhaps you would find it helpful to hear how God could surmount, even use, the evil circumstances in one life, and bring great good out of them. Perhaps your life is similarly plagued. If so, I do not know what God has in store for you, but if you are faithful, God may bring good out of your circumstances, too.

The greatest obstacle God had to overcome in my early years was pride. You see, I had been raised under the doting care of my father, Jacob. Sometimes he is also called Israel. He was a sheik — a wandering shepherd chieftain in the land of Canaan. He had four wives, but my mother, Rachel, was the love of his life. In all, my father had twelve children, but only two by Rachel. I was the first one born to Rachel, so I was his favorite. My father never tried to hide his favoritism, and so I naturally assumed that somehow I was superior to my brothers. I got easier work, and I stayed around the tent when my brothers went out to pasture their sheep. I'm afraid I did not have the good sense to be humble about these blessings, and I tried to lord it over my brothers. To make matters worse, my father gave me a coat of many colors — a sign of authority — a badge of special preference — and I wore it for all it was worth.

17

Beyond that, I had premonitions of a great destiny. And like a fool, I never let my family forget it. You see, I periodically had dreams which spoke for themselves. I dreamed once that we were binding stacks of grain in the field, when suddenly my stack stood erect and each of my brothers' stacks bowed before it. In my usually arrogant manner, I told my brothers the dream and they said, "Do you really expect to reign over us?" I had another dream in which the sun, moon and eleven stars bowed before me. When I told that, even my father couldn't take it. He said, "Shall your brothers and even your father and mother bow before you? Come, come now, Joseph." My father dismissed it, but my brothers were consumed with jealousy.

As is so often the case with those who are blessed, I was completely oblivious to my brothers' feelings. That brought me to my first disaster. When I was seventeen years old, my brothers happened to be pasturing the sheep several days journey from our home. My father wanted to know how things were going with my ten older brothers, so he sent me to find out. When I was still some distance from their camp, my brothers saw me and conspired to kill me. Reuben, my oldest brother, was not sold on the idea, however, and he persuaded the rest to throw me into a dry well to die of thirst. I learned years later that he had intended to come and get me out. Judah, another brother, didn't want my blood on his hands either, so when a caravan of Midianite traders passed by, he suggested that I be sold to them as a slave. They all agreed to that, and I was carried off to Egypt. I learned years later that my brothers dipped my coat of many colors in goat's blood and brought it to my father to convince him that I had been killed by a wild beast. I could only see the dark prospect of slavery before me at the time, but I now have sufficient insight to ask, "Was it just fate that a caravan happened to come by, and thus save my life?"

The second phase of my life takes place in Egypt. I was sold to Potiphar, a captain of Pharaoh's guard. At first I did menial tasks, but Potiphar took a liking to me, and put me in charge of his whole household. My authority was next to his own. It was not like being at home, but it was better than a slave could have expected. My misfortunes had taught me humility; my new position taught me responsibility, and I was grateful to Potiphar.

There was a fly in the ointment, however. Potiphar, being a soldier, was away a good deal, and his attractive wife became bored. For want of anything better to do, she began to make advances toward me, at first in jest, but then in dead earnest. I could not bring myself to violate Potiphar's trust in me, however, and I resisted her every appeal. Her advances became more and more overt, until one day she grabbed my coat and I couldn't think of anything else to save us from our passions, so I ran out. She felt rebuffed, perhaps ashamed, and determined to get back at me, so she called in the servants and showed them my coat, saying that I had tried to assault her. I know what you're thinking. I see that knowing look in everybody's eyes when I tell them that part of the story. They think that either I did try to assault her and failed, or that if I'm telling the truth, I shouldn't have been as pure as all that. You know, people are always talking about virtue and integrity, but when they meet someone who has resisted temptation, when it would have been easier to yield, they don't really believe it could happen.

Well, of course she told Potiphar, and he had me thrown in prison. Since he was an officer in the palace guard he had me placed in the royal prison, where I was confined with the king's own prisoners — there to await my fate. What more could happen to me — alone, a slave, imprisoned in a foreign country, awaiting death? That prison was my home for years. Perhaps Potiphar forgot about me, or perhaps he had suspicions about his wife and chose to proceed no farther. I, in any case, was left to rot.

While I was in prison, however, the warden took notice of me and made me a trustee. In fact, he put me in charge of all the prisoners. This wasn't like being in Potiphar's house, but if one had to be in prison, this was the best way. While I was there, the king became angry with his chief butler and chief baker and had them thrown into prison. I came to know them well. One night, each of them had a dream, and they were troubled because they could not understand their dreams. When I heard the dreams, God gave me the power to interpret them. I told the baker that in three days he would be executed, and the butler that in three days he would be restored to the king's service. Each was dealt with as I had said. I asked the butler to remember me before the king when he was restored, but he did not. Yet, in the light of what subsequently happened, I must ask: Was it just fate that I was accused falsely by Potiphar's wife? Was it just fate that I was thrown into the king's own prison, that I met his servants, heard their dreams, interpreted them rightly? I am convinced it was more than fate.

The third part of my story deals with how I became Prime Minister of all Egypt. Two years after the butler's release, Pharaoh had two dreams. In one he saw seven skinny cows eat seven fat ones and get no larger. In the other he saw seven empty ears of grain eat seven full ears of grain. He sought for interpretation and could find none. Then it was that the butler remembered his experience and told Pharaoh of me. Pharaoh sent for me and demanded interpretation. I told him that if the interpretation came, it would be from God alone. As Pharaoh told me his dreams, their meaning became obvious to me. The good grain and cattle stood for seven years of plenty. The poor grain and cattle stood for seven years of famine that would devour what was stored in the good years. I made the interpretation known and advised Pharaoh to appoint a minister of agriculture to gather surplus grain for the lean years ahead. Of all persons, Pharaoh appointed me! He gave me unlimited authority to gather grain, and bestowed upon me the titles I mentioned earlier.

Little did I realize that my greatest test was still before me. When the famine came, it struck all of the Middle East. People came from near and far to buy grain. And among them all, one day, stood my ten brothers. After twenty years, they had fallen into my hands. They did not recognize me, but bowed down, begging permission to buy grain. I did not know what I would do with them. I thought I would test them to see if they had changed any. Through my interpreter I accused them of being spies. They insisted that they were ten brothers, that one was dead and that another younger one was at home. I said the only way I would believe them was if they could produce the other brother who was still at home. They could buy grain, I said, but one would have to remain as hostage until the rest returned with the younger brother. I wanted to see Benjamin again, for he was the only other one born to my mother.

They bemoaned their fate, and I heard them say that this had befallen them because of their treatment of me years before. I gave them further cause for alarm by having their money put back in their grain sacks.

In time they returned to me with our youngest brother, Benjamin, and I released Simeon, whom I had detained. They said their father would die if anything happened to Benjamin. I wanted to see if they would be more noble toward Benjamin than they had been toward me, so I had my own silver cup put in Benjamin's sack of grain. When they had left, I sent soldiers after them to apprehend the one who had taken my cup. They all returned, and Judah pleaded with me to punish him and let Benjamin go. I could no longer contain myself, and in tears of joy I revealed who I was. They were seized with guilt and fully expected I would kill them all in revenge. Instead, I pleaded with them to bring my father and all their families to live with me in Egypt. They did just that.

We were happy together for years, and my father died happy at a good old age. Then my brothers began to fear again that perhaps I had only spared them for my father's sake and that I would now take revenge. It was then that I told them what I had learned about the hand of God: "Fear not, for while you meant evil against me, God meant it for good, to bring it about that many people should be kept alive."

Perhaps you have been wondering why I am telling you all this. I simply want to point out that things may look bad while they are happening, as indeed they did for me when I was thrown into a pit, when I was sold into slavery, when Potiphar's wife got me undeserved disgrace, and when I lay in Pharaoh's prison. But try to view things from the other end, too. Who brought the caravan by at the right time? Why was I placed in a royal prison? What brought me to the attention of Pharaoh's servant, and consequently to Pharaoh? Good people could not have made these things happen, nor could bad people have prevented them. God was at work in all of this. I don't believe that God *brings* bad situations on us — but God can *use* them. I don't say God *always* brings good out of evil, but I do think that if we continue to trust God, we will be able to look back and see that God really has been with us, even when we did not know it.

21

3. The Desert Fox

Exodus 3:1-14

People often have a rather elevated view of leaders. They tend to regard leaders as persons who are larger than life. Leaders are thought to be people of unique talents presented with unique opportunities. Often people will say, "If only I had been born back in *those* days, I might have done something." "If only I had more physical strength, or more money, or more education, I might do something significant." I know that is the way people think about leadership, because I have felt that way myself. And I'm here to tell you that just isn't the way it is. Most people have what it takes to do something significant. They just don't realize it, and consequently, they discount what they have to contribute. There are others who really don't want the hard work of doing what needs to be done, and their suggestion that they lack something is only an excuse. I can say that because I have experienced both of those feelings, and yet leadership became my lot anyway. I think I can safely say that no matter what your experiences have been, God can use them.

My name is Moses. Let me tell you how it was with me. I think my experiences can have application to your life.

I was a simple shepherd out in the Arabian desert of Sinai. I was so poor that I didn't even have my own flock. I took care of the sheep for my father-in-law, Jethro, who, in addition to owning the sheep, happened to be a tribal holy man, a priest, who worshiped the Most High God. I only had the job because I had married one of his daughters, Zipporah. Jethro and I had a good relationship, and I was quite content to be out with the sheep day after day. The work was not demanding, I had few responsibilities, and I had a lot of time to think.

I had, in fact, been shepherding for a good many years in the vicinity of Mount Horeb, or Sinai, as some call it, when the incident I am about to describe took place. I was looking for a missing lamb on the slopes of Mount Sinai when I chanced to look up and see a bush that looked like it was on fire, only the bush didn't burn. It may have been the result of a small eruption, for Sinai was an active volcano and was often belching forth smoke. It was while I was observing this phenomenon that I felt overwhelmed by the presence of Something I could not explain. I felt that I had somehow intruded on holy ground. I felt as though I was carrying on a conversation with Something or Someone I couldn't see. I say I *felt* these things because I'm not sure whether I heard them with my ears or whether they made an impact on my mind in some other way — but I am sure what the message was.

I was being asked to go to Egypt to lead the Hebrews out of captivity. Now you may not know what I am talking about, because I haven't told you everything about my background. You see, I am a Hebrew. My people had gone down into Egypt some several hundred years before and lived as a minority among the Egyptians. Eventually my people became slaves of Pharaoh, king of Egypt. We became numerous enough that Pharaoh feared what might happen if we ever joined forces with an enemy of Egypt, so he tried several means of reducing our population growth. One of his methods was to require that all Hebrew boy babies be drowned in the Nile. When I was born, that was supposed to have happened to me. Instead, my parents put me in a waterproof basket and put me on the river with my sister, Miriam, standing by. I was found by Pharaoh's daughter and raised as her own son. My birth mother managed to become my nursemaid, and she acquainted me with my true heritage.

I was raised as an Egyptian noble and trained in the wisdom of Egypt. My people were suffering cruelly, but there was nothing I could do. One day I saw an Egyptian taskmaster beating one of the Hebrews, and in my attempt to stop him, I killed the Egyptian. I tried to keep it a secret, but in no time the Hebrews knew about it, and since many of them considered me a traitor for living in the palace, I knew that it was only a question of time before someone would inform on me, so I fled Egypt in a panic.

I came to the area of Sinai seeking refuge, and Jethro, the Midianite, took me in. That is why I was quite content to serve out there on the desert in relative anonymity. You can understand, then, why I would not want to go back to Egypt. But the call was insistent; it wouldn't leave me alone. I protested that there must be others who could do it better. I said I didn't know enough. I didn't even know who I was talking to. The voice, whether inside me or outside of me, I don't know, said, "I am the God of your forefathers." I said, "The people will want to know your name." The voice answered, "I am Yahweh," a Hebrew word which might mean a variety of things, like "I am what I am," or "The one who brings into existence what is." I protested that the people wouldn't listen to me. I protested my lack of ability, my lack of eloquence as a speaker. Finally, I said, "I don't *want* to go. I'm comfortable here. Get someone else." But nothing would remove the sense of urgency; Yahweh was commissioning me to go, and in the final analysis I felt compelled to obey. I was not a volunteer; I was drafted. I was not a religious fanatic; I had scarcely paid any heed to God previously. I was not a political reformer; I really wanted to be left alone. But I was called, and if I did not respond, I could not continue to live with myself.

Now you may think I have forgotten my main point, which is to draw lessons from my life which might apply to you, but I haven't forgotten. For one thing, I am sure that there are still people in *your* day who need to be delivered, as Israel needed to be delivered in *my* day. Some need deliverance from physical hunger and poverty. Some need deliverance from slavery to dehumanizing habits. Others need deliverance from hatred and violence which kills body and spirit. Still others need deliverance from obsession with material accumulation which blots out spiritual values.

Another way your life relates to mine is that *you* are called to help with the deliverance in *your* time just as *I* was in *my* time. You may protest that there are all kinds of reasons why you are not the person for the job, just as I did, but when all the pretense has been stripped away, you may be faced with the fact, as I was, that the *real* obstacle is simply that you don't want to get involved. All of us tend to think that there must be somebody else somewhere who can do more than we can to correct a bad situation, and so we claim that it isn't our concern. The fact is that most people who do something significant aren't necessarily more talented than anyone else, they just got in there and did what needed to be done, using whatever resources were at their disposal. If you wait around for the perfect person to show up to do a job, someone who has all the right qualifications, the job isn't going to get done.

I certainly didn't have much to offer, but I had been given a vision of the task to be done, and that became the call of God for me. And don't tell me that is where the difference lies between you and me — that God spoke to me but he has not spoken to you. If you have seen injustice, and you can recognize it, if you have seen poverty, hunger, misery, illness, hate, war, fear, pain, and you can recognize these things as bad, then you have received the call to help correct them. A call begins with an awareness that things could be different. Of that much I was aware. So I was compelled to do what I could with the tools available to me. Those tools didn't seem like much, but God used them.

One of the tools, if you want to call them that, was my ancestry. I was a Hebrew, so I was already identified with the problems of the Hebrews. They were my people, and I had an obligation to help. That meant I had to be where they were. I couldn't help them without taking the risk of putting myself in jeopardy. I had to become part of their circumstances, even face possible arrest. Even when you feel called, there is a price to pay for the privilege of helping.

You, too, have an ancestry. It may be ethnic, national, religious, or simply your identity with all humanity. Where are your people hurting? That's one way to hear your call. But before you can help, you've got to identify with those who need the help.

I went back to Egypt. I lived among my people. My brother, Aaron, often served as my spokesman. I had to raise the consciousness of my people to a level where they were willing to act, and that often made me unpopular, even with my own people.

Another tool I had going for me was contact with the power structure. I had been raised as an Egyptian. I knew their language. I knew their organization. I knew some of their principal people in government. I knew what was likely to impress them. I went to them and told them that my people needed to be free to make a three-day journey into the desert to worship our God.

You may say that right there I had an advantage that you don't have: the opportunity to go to the top. But think that over. Aren't there ways for you to contact important people? In fact, isn't it possible for you to get involved in the process of putting people in the places of power? You may feel that they won't listen to you, but don't be too sure. It is important to speak out. They didn't seem to listen to me either. Even so, I engaged in a process of consciousness raising.

Still another tool I could offer in the accomplishment of God's purpose was my awareness of natural phenomena. I used this knowledge to bring our desire for freedom more dramatically to the attention of Pharaoh, his advisers, and the Egyptians in general. I told them that our God had called us to worship him some three-days' journey into the desert. Really, that was to help Pharaoh save face. Certainly, we had no intention of returning to slavery if we ever got away. I knew that, and Pharaoh knew that, but he would have had to be even more resistant to an outright demand to free my people permanently.

Periodically, in the past, the Nile River would crest high up at its source and tend to bring a red algae down from the mountains. This tended to turn the Nile red like blood. I had learned about this when I was tutored in the palace. I saw signs of that beginning to happen, so I said that Pharaoh must let our people go or the Nile would turn to blood. He refused to let us go, and shortly thereafter the river turned red. Pharaoh was not impressed, but I had at least gotten his attention.

There were also natural consequences of this reddening that I knew would take place: the fish would die; frogs would come out of the river; the frogs would die; this would attract flies; flies would infect animals and people, and so forth. Before each of these events took place I would seek out and inform Pharaoh in as public a way as I could, that he must let my people go, but each time he refused. My people, living in a different area, were not exposed to these plagues, and consequently, they were spared.

You may think that this knowledge of natural phenomena discredits God's involvement and takes things out of the realm of the supernatural. I say, not at all. All knowledge is from God. When ignorant people see something they can't explain, they call it magic. I prefer to call it "miracle." A miracle is something that we can't presently explain, but it has an explanation. God does not delight in ignorance, but in knowledge. The more we learn, and the more we use what we learn for the benefit of others, the more we are in tune with God's intention.

There was also something the Egyptians were doing which was having a devastating effect on their children, so that many of their children died. It was not so among us, and I saw that this contrast would finally force the Egyptians to want to be rid of us. So I told my people to get ready, to be packed and prepared to travel, because I didn't want to give the Egyptians the chance to reconsider, once they decided to let us go. Not knowing myself what caused the deaths of the Egyptian children, I told my people first to sacrifice a lamb, and then to make a mark on their door posts with the blood to signify to the angel of death that Hebrews lived there. The night before we departed we had a hasty meal, which we have subsequently repeated each year, to remember our release from slavery. We call it the Passover, for the angel of death passed over our homes.

Once we left Egypt, God continued to help me to use my knowledge to keep the Hebrews free and to keep them alive. Our journey led to a shallow extension of the Red Sea called the Sea of Reeds. No sooner had we arrived there than Pharaoh's army showed up with the intention of bringing us back. He had changed his mind! We had no choice but to move ahead. The sea was shallow enough so that a strong wind blowing on the surface of the water made it possible for us to pick our way and proceed on foot. Pharaoh's heavy chariots and galloping horses, however, became mired in the mud and had to give up.

So, crossing the sea, we found ourselves in territory with which I was familiar. I knew where there were some oases for refreshment. I knew how to make bitter water drinkable by throwing a certain kind of wood into it. I knew where one could find underground springs with a little digging. I knew about migrations of quail which could provide meat. I knew about the secretions of the tamarisk tree which provided adequate nutrition: a food my people called "manna," meaning simply "what is it?"

What I had to offer was simple, just a shepherd's knowledge, but it was what was needed at that particular moment, and it kept my people alive. Do not think I am saying that "Moses did this or that." It was God who called me when I did not want to go. It was the God of nature who had created the natural laws that helped us. It was God's nearness to me that made it possible for me to put up with the never-ending complaints my own people had about all that I did. Undoubtedly you, too, have something God can use to advance God's purposes for the world.

The last tool I'll tell you about, which I had to offer for God's use, was my ability to make things simple. Sometimes people who are put into positions of leadership act as though their calling is to make an idea as unintelligible as possible. Nobody ever knows what they are talking about, and it is impossible to disagree with them. I, on the other hand, am a simple man, and I appreciate things being done or described in a simple way. After all, most of my life was spent as a simple shepherd out in the desert of Sinai. Now I was once again a shepherd, only this time my flock was people instead of sheep. In the years which remained to me I was to have the responsibility for taking a downtrodden people with little self-confidence and building them into a unified nation, with a sense of national pride and an awareness of their destiny. At the moment, however, they were fighting with me and with one another, and were completely unaware of any responsibility for their conduct or their future. There was stealing, lying, cheating, unfaithfulness, jealousy, and all manner of social evils that would destroy us quickly. Something had to be done to make us aware of our higher calling.

I had received my call in the vicinity of Mount Sinai, and it was to that area that we were slowly making our way. When we arrived there, after a journey of some months, the mountain was again erupting, and I told the people that was the way it had been when God had spoken to me before. The people urged me to go up into the mountain and to speak with God. I went up, and I spent forty days away from the camp. I needed the rest, I needed time to think, and I needed the quietness of mind, body, and spirit, which would enable me to hear the voice of God. As I spent time on the mountain, it became abundantly clear what my people needed. First, they needed to commit themselves unreservedly to the God who had brought them out of slavery. They needed to be aware that God is a spiritual reality who would be present with them wherever they might go. They needed to be aware that God had chosen them for a great destiny and that they were free to accept or reject that invitation, but that once they accepted it, they would be expected to organize their lives in a manner which God could approve. I set these thoughts down on stone in the simplest manner: just ten phrases to serve as an outline of the kind of life of which God could approve, the kind of contract that we would be expected to live up to. I don't claim that these concepts were new or unique with me, or that I am the only one through whom God could speak. All I can say is that as I humbly reflected on my people's needs, these were the ideas which God put into my mind. About all that I contributed was the simplicity of organizing them.

When I came down from the mountain with the two tablets of the law, I found that my people were already involved in breaking the very laws I had just written down! In anger and despair I smashed the two stone tablets together, symbolizing even more than I intended, the fact that they were breaking God's law. When they learned the nature of my message, they pleaded with me to pray to God for forgiveness and to ask that the law be put down once again. I did as they requested. God forgave; the law was written again, and the people accepted its implications for their lives.

There is much more I could tell you of our experiences as we learned to be God's people. But what I want you to be aware of even more than our story is how God can use the simplest characteristics you have to offer and make something of them. The key, of course, is that you have to be ready to use what God has given you. You need to ask yourself: What are the issues in my day calling for solution? What do I have that could contribute to a solution? What do I know, or need to learn, that would help? Is there something in particular that God wants me to be concerned about? And don't wait for a burning bush to catch your attention. That was my unique experience. You just listen, with your mind and your heart, and when you hear the call, be prepared to say, "Yes."

4. The Complaining Prophet

Jeremiah 7:1-7

I can still remember the words which started me out on my unwilling journey: "Before I formed you in the womb I knew you, and before you were born I consecrated you; I appointed you a prophet to the nations." It was God who was speaking to me. Oh, how I wished that the words were not addressed to me! I tried to avoid the call. I said, "I am only a youth." After all, I was only about nineteen. But God said, "I will be with you and deliver you." I then countered that I didn't know how to speak, but God touched my mouth and said, "Behold, I have put my words in your mouth."

Perhaps you think that it would be exciting to be a prophet. Well, after forty years as a spokesman for God, I can tell you that it has not been an easy experience: pain, agony, sorrow, sadness, abuse, punishment, rejection, isolation, these things have all been a part of it. But there has been nothing in the role that one would seek if he had the choice. Many times I would have given up this task, but I could not; I was compelled to speak.

Soon after the call came to me, it was confirmed by a vision. I saw a boiling pot with steam being blown from the north, and I heard God saying, "Out of the north, evil shall break forth on the inhabitants of the land." This meant to me that a military power from the north was going to fall upon my people, Judah, and that I was commissioned to provide the warning. I was told that I would meet with opposition from kings, princes, priests, and people, but that I must speak what God commanded, and God would be with me.

My name is Jeremiah. I am from the little village of Anathoth, about two miles north of Jerusalem. I was told to go to Jerusalem to proclaim my message, which I understood was to bring the people back to God.

I thought it best to discover for myself how the people were living so that I could speak from knowledge. What I discovered

31

appalled me! I walked through the streets of Jerusalem and discovered that the people were lying, faithless, and unjust to one another. At first I thought that perhaps it was only the ignorant and poor who did not know God's law, but I found that it was the same among the prominent. I understood that punishment would be inevitable if the people did not change their ways.

The outcome for my people would eventually prove to be a sad one, but perhaps what I learned during my ministry could have some value for you, for people in every age need to evaluate themselves.

One thing I learned is that true religion is not dependent on institutional ritual. My people thought of themselves as unique because they had been the recipients of God's law. But it was obvious from their lifestyle that they did not know God's law. My people had *heard* the law, but it could not save them, for they did not practice it. Perhaps you, too, know how you should live, but that is no help to you if you don't practice it.

Others were relying unduly on religious rituals. They thought that by the abundance of their sacrifices and the intricacy of their religious observances they could please God. I told them that God was not impressed by sacrifices, but by obedience. God is an ethical being. It was not God who had set up Israel's elaborate system of worship. People had done that, and as a result they had diverted attention from what was absolutely essential to the worship of God: moral obedience.

Consider, for example, the practice of circumcision. It was a mark on our bodies that we were the people of God; and many felt that it ensured God's protection. I told them that the outward mark of circumcision was utterly worthless. It had been intended to signify spiritual dependence and amended lives, but it had come to signify nothing. What was needed was a circumcised heart! A ritual wasn't going to save anyone if it didn't reflect an inner attitude. Perhaps there are rituals that you have been relying on that also need to be reexamined in order to discover their original meaning.

The time I really got into trouble was when I spoke against the temple. You see, religious people tend to think that the place where they worship is the dwelling place of God. My people had been worshiping in the temple for 350 years; it had become hallowed by tradition. I stood up in the court of the temple and told them that the temple wasn't going to save anyone. God could not abide with his people, no matter how ardent their love for the temple, if they oppressed the helpless in society and continued to steal, murder, lie, and gouge one another in the market place. What God desired was morally transformed conduct.

They believed that the temple was some kind of talisman, and that its very presence would protect them from all harm. I told them that if they did not change their ways, God himself would destroy that holy place and send them off to exile. That was going too far for those in authority. The prophets and the priests seized me and accused me of blasphemy. They said that I should die. I insisted that I was speaking only as the Lord had instructed me, and that my purpose was to bring the people to repentance.

They let me go, but I was a marked man; informers eagerly reported what I said, assassinations were attempted, even my own family threatened me, for I was an embarrassment to them. I was hurt, confused, frightened, but nevertheless determined to make my people see what would surely happen if they did not change. I took a pottery jar and broke it before a small crowd at the gate of the city, and I said, "In just such a manner will the Lord break the people of this city into pieces, because they refuse to hear the word of the Lord." When I spoke again in the temple area, Pashhur, one of the temple officers, had me arrested, beaten, and placed in stocks for 24 hours because, he said, I was falsely exercising a prophet's function. In every age, people who do not like what God is saying to them will do all in their power to shut up God's word, even as I was shut up in stocks.

When I was released, I was forbidden to enter the temple area. I cursed the day that I was born, that I should find myself in this predicament. I hadn't *asked* for this job; it was thrust upon me. I didn't *want* to be the bearer of evil tidings; I didn't *enjoy* bringing bad news. Nevertheless, I was suffering because of it. I felt that God had seduced me, used me for his purposes, and abandoned me. I decided to keep silent, but the words became a burning fire in my bones; I had to speak.

About that time I was led to take another approach. I received a revelation that I should write down the contents of my preaching ministry up to that point. I hoped that the cumulative effect of my words might succeed where my messages individually had failed. I hoped that my people might return to God and be forgiven. So I dictated my sermons to my friend, Baruch, and then asked him to go and read the words of the scroll publicly in the temple, for I was forbidden to go there. Some nobles got hold of the scroll and had it read before the king. In an effort to demonstrate his utter contempt for the word of the Lord, the king cut off every few columns of the scroll as it was read, and threw the pieces into the fire. There was now no hope for Judah. I could and did write a new scroll, but I could not make the people or the king change their ways. They were depending on religious institutions, which could not save them.

A second thing that I learned is that true religion is not dependent upon national survival. My people felt that our nation was special, that it would always survive. They could quote the promises of some of the past prophets who had spoken of such survival. The problem was that they didn't take seriously the conditions of those promises: that they must live just and upright lives, serving the Lord.

There was no reason to think we were God's pet any longer. More than 100 years before, the Assyrians had swooped down on our sister kingdom, Israel, and taken her people into exile. When that was pointed out to my people, they said, in effect, "Ah, yes, but those people really were unrighteous, and God was punishing them." Somehow, my people couldn't get the message that this could happen to them too.

In 605 B.C. we lost a major battle with Nebuchadrezzar, King of Babylon, and we became tributary to him. It became clear to me that Babylon was "the foe from the north," which I had seen in my first vision. I urged the king and people not to provoke Nebuchadrezzar, so that things would go well with us, for I saw him as the unwitting instrument of God, sent to correct us and to cause us to examine our lives.

My preaching was to no avail. At the urging of Egypt, our king stopped paying tribute, and in 597 Nebuchadrezzar defeated our forces, captured our city, and took the king and 10,000 of our leading citizens into exile in Babylon. A new king was put on the throne, but our cities were left intact. In no time, the people were again discussing rebellion. They were so hopeful that the exiles would return, that they listened to anyone who said it would be soon. And the prophets and priests told them what they wanted to hear. I could see that the exile would be long, and that my people had better forget this talk of rebellion, or the Babylonians would come and utterly destroy our land and take more people into captivity.

They would not listen. In time, the foreign ministers of some of the small powers around us gathered in Jerusalem for a secret conference to discuss revolt. I felt led to become a demonstrator. I put a wooden yoke on my neck and paraded all through the city, saying that we had better recognize the situation that we were in: that the Lord of creation had allowed this to come to pass and that we had better learn to live peaceably under this yoke. Of course, that was not a popular message, but the people needed to hear it. Hananiah, one of the prophets who wanted war, took the yoke from my neck and broke it in pieces, saying, "Thus says the Lord: 'Like this will I break the yoke of the king of Babylon within two years from the neck of all the nations.' " I responded that nothing would please me more, but it was not to be, for Hananiah's words did not take into account Judah's moral condition. Time would bear out who was right.

Eventually, the worst happened. The king was persuaded to revolt. Judah was attacked, her towns destroyed, and Jerusalem surrounded by Babylonian troops. By now, the king had come to believe that I did, indeed, speak the word of the Lord, but he was not able to stand against the contrary opinion of the nobles, who were against me, and who sought to destroy me. I told him and all who would listen that we should surrender, or Jerusalem would be destroyed.

Now they became concerned for social justice and gave orders that all slaves should be freed. They said they did it to please God. In reality, those who owned slaves could no longer afford to feed them in a besieged city, so the reason for releasing the slaves was really economic. About that time Egypt made a weak gesture of coming to our aid, and the siege was lifted. The people thought they were delivered, and the first thing they did was to put their slaves back into bondage.

The Babylonians returned and we were once again laid under siege. This time I knew that the end had come for our beloved city. Still, I wanted to show my people that there could be hope for the future. An incident which occurred about that time helped me to make the point. A cousin, who owned property in Anathoth, was in need of money, and sought to sell me the property, even though it was now occupied by foreign troops. I accepted the opportunity, and had the deed publicly notarized and publicly filed, for it was my way of saying that one day houses and fields and vineyards would again be sold in the land. I, who had been so pessimistic, felt that I now needed to demonstrate some hope.

Eventually, the city was taken, everything in it was destroyed, thousands more were taken into exile, and Judah and Jerusalem were absorbed into the Babylonian Empire. Because I had urged my people not to revolt I was allowed to remain in the land with some few others who were to till the soil and care for crops. That was not the end of things. In this calamity I had already discovered that true religion is not based on institutional ritual. Now I understood that true religion is not dependent on the survival of the nation either.

The third thing that I discovered is that true religion is an affair of the heart. God showed me that one day he would set up a new covenant with his people. Not like the old covenant, written on tablets of stone, which the people received at Sinai. That covenant always had about it requirement and obligation: it was something imposed from outside the person. But the new covenant would be written on the hearts of individuals. God would put his law in the innermost being of a person, so that to know the law would be to do it.

A time was coming when people would recognize that the Lord is not the God of the Jews only, but the God of all creation. They would see that the Lord is not tied to one land or one temple, for God may be worshiped by anyone, anywhere, when God is worshiped from the heart.

I know that true religion is an affair of the heart, because God granted me a foretaste of that kind of religion in my own life. He called me personally and I responded. That doesn't mean we were always in agreement, however. You may recall, I didn't want the job in the first place. But such was our relationship that God did not abandon me. We were friends, and I was permitted to express myself, for it was a relationship of love.

It was that personal relationship which sustained me when all the familiar landmarks of nation and religion were disappearing. I believe that such a relationship can also sustain you, whatever you are called upon to endure. You may be strengthened in trouble, but do not expect such a relationship to protect you from trouble; I certainly did not find that. And do not expect always to understand what God is seeking to do, for in the final analysis God is sovereign, and we are God's subjects. That was brought home forcefully to me by one further experience I had. And with this I close.

I happened to go into a pottery shop one day, and I observed the potter making a vessel from a lump of clay. He had almost completed the vessel, when some imperfection was found in it. Undismayed, he mashed the marred vessel into a lump again, set the wheel turning, and worked the clay into another vessel which met with his approval. At that moment a new insight dawned upon my mind. It was the realization that Judah, although it was a spoiled vessel, was still in the hands of God, a God of infinite resourcefulness, and of abiding, enduring love. God's intention for his people had been frustrated, but not defeated. The Divine Potter still loved his clay. Whether we are talking about Judah or about any people, God has an intention for us. It may be temporarily thwarted because of our imperfections, but one day God will use all that we are or have been to bring his purpose to pass. If we want to be part of that purpose, what we have to do is to cooperate.

5. Mary's Song

Luke 1:5-56

Some mighty strange things have happened in our family during the past few months. I don't know where it will all come out, but all of us are pretty sure that what happened will be significant for all Israel. My name is Zechariah. I am a priest of God Most High. What happened to my wife and to me is incredible enough, but what happened to another member of our family is even more amazing. Allow me to tell you about it.

Almost a year ago I had come up to Jerusalem to serve in the temple for a week. You see, in all Israel there are so many priests that we have been divided into 24 divisions. Each division serves in the temple for one week twice a year. The remainder of our time we spend attending to religious matters in our hometowns. Even when we go up to Jerusalem, there are so many of us that only a few of us can enter the holy place to burn incense before God. Naturally, it is an honor that each of us seeks, so we cast lots to decide who will be chosen to burn the incense each day. It is a great privilege for a priest to be able to go into such a holy place and pray to God on behalf of the people.

Well, on the particular day I want to talk about, the lot fell to me to enter the holy place to burn incense. I had had the opportunity before, but even so, it was an exciting prospect. As I entered the temple, people were already kneeling in prayer all around the outside, waiting for the incense symbolically to carry their prayers heavenward. I couldn't help but think that it would have been nice if my wife Elizabeth could have been present to observe this great moment, but it was the custom that priests' wives should remain at home.

As I prepared the incense, I prayed for the people, although I suppose there also went through my mind that prayer that Elizabeth and I had so often uttered: the prayer that we might have a child. I don't think I consciously dwelt on it, for Elizabeth and I are now old. I am getting ready to retire, and there was no longer any expectation of children for us. It was at that very moment that a vision appeared just to one side of the altar. I don't know what else to call it but an angel, a messenger from God. Now I know that sounds crazy. Most people are pretty skeptical when I tell them about it, but that's not half what I was. I was scared right out of my wits. The angel said, "Don't be afraid, Zechariah, your prayer is heard." I thought to myself, "That's good. I've been an effective priest." But the angel continued, "Your wife Elizabeth will bear you a son, and you shall call his name John." So *that* was the prayer that was heard. Here I was supposed to be serving the people, and apparently, I had been serving myself. The angel continued. He spoke of the joy Elizabeth and I would know. Well, if a birth really occurred, joy would be putting it mildly. He said our son would be filled with the Holy Spirit and that he would turn many people to God.

My fear began to turn to disbelief. I thought to myself, "Who is going to believe this?" In the first place, my wife and I are too old to have children. So I said, "Give me some proof that this will take place or I won't even have the courage to tell my wife about it." The angel presented his credentials. It was Gabriel himself. He found it inconceivable that I should question what he was telling me, so he said, "Very well, your proof will be the fact that you won't be able to tell anyone. You will be unable to speak until the child is born." Then he vanished.

When I came outside, all the people were waiting for me to give some kind of a blessing. I opened my mouth, but nothing came out. I made signs with my hands and the people understood that I had seen a vision. There was considerable speculation among the other priests as to what had happened in the holy place. Some thought I had had a stroke. When our week was up, I returned home.

Of course, Elizabeth was concerned that I couldn't speak. When I wrote out for her what I had been told, she was ecstatic. Sure enough, in due time she conceived, and then, as women will, she did a strange thing. She refused to be seen for five months. I guess after so many years of waiting, she wanted to be absolutely certain that she was pregnant before she showed herself to the townspeople.

In Elizabeth's sixth month we had a visitor, Elizabeth's young cousin, Mary of Nazareth. If you think what happened to us was strange, wait till you hear about Mary! No sooner had Mary entered our home than Elizabeth's unborn child began to leap within her. And Elizabeth herself broke out in a cry of prophecy. She blessed Mary, and she blessed Mary's eventual children, she blessed Mary's faith. She expressed her own unworthiness that the mother of her "Lord" should visit her. I didn't understand the meaning of that last part.

It turned out that we were not the only ones with news; Mary had a few things to tell us too. Just a few days earlier Mary also had had a vision. The same heavenly messenger, Gabriel, came to her as he had come to me. She, too, was to give birth to a son. She, too, was given the name for her son. It was to be Jesus, which means "God Is Salvation." She was told that her son was to be great, that he would be called Son of God, that he would set up an eternal kingdom. All this was to come about, she was told, through the power of the Holy Spirit. The proof that this was going to take place was the fact that her cousin, Elizabeth, after all those years of waiting, was going to have a child. That was how Mary had learned of Elizabeth's condition. She had come to see for herself, and to help if she could.

Here was this poor teenage girl, not much more than sixteen, not yet married, and she was pregnant. Whatever the circumstances, she needed all the love and support she could get. She was engaged to Joseph, a carpenter in their hometown of Nazareth. She hadn't yet told him that she was pregnant. What a shock that was going to be! Now I must confess that I was pretty skeptical of what she was telling us. Thank God my tongue was silent so that I couldn't say what I was thinking.

Mary stayed with us for several months, leaving just before our child was born. I was amazed that all of this could be going on in one family. But I also began to see God's wisdom in all this. Through our similar circumstances we could support each other in looking for the meaning of what we were experiencing. During the several months Mary was with us, we tried to help her work through her difficult situation. We talked much about the strange things that were befalling our family, and we spent many evenings exploring our heritage to look for situations that paralleled our own. I couldn't speak, but I certainly could write. One of the things that immediately suggested itself to us was the experience of Hannah, which was recorded for us in the First Book of Samuel. Hannah was a married woman, but she was barren. She suffered great reproach because of her barrenness. She prayed to the Lord for a child, and the Lord heard her prayer and caused her to conceive a child who became Samuel, one of our great leaders, the last of the judges and the first of the prophets. When Hannah received the news, she glorified God with a lovely poem that eventually became a song for the whole congregation of Israel. Her circumstances were more akin to those of mine and Elizabeth's, but I had to acknowledge that if what Mary was telling us were true, then her child would have an even more significant destiny than Hannah's child or ours.

More or less to amuse Mary, and to get her mind off of the social repercussions she was likely to experience when she returned to Nazareth, I urged her to write down her thoughts, and I gave her a copy of Hannah's song as a model to follow. That young girl's words convinced me of her sincerity and made it apparent to me that her child would be someone special. Her song — I think you could call it that — expressed devout praise for God, who, she insisted, had done great things for her, exalting her low estate, and making her a participant in something great.

One part of her message was good news. She said that in this event God was exalting the humble. God knows we could stand that kind of message for a change. It always seems to be the powerful who are making the decisions that affect the poor and keep the poor poor. The powerful decide to go to war, and it is the poor, simple folk who do the fighting and who have their homes and families destroyed. To be told that the lowly can take responsibility for their own destiny would truly be revolutionary.

She said that the hungry will be filled with good things. So many of the people in God's world are hungry that they have come

42

to see hunger as normative. Many have given up the idea of ever experiencing a full stomach. To be told that this is not God's intention, that it doesn't have to be that way, that God intends for his children to be full, gives hungry people a dignity they did not know they had. It restores hope to God's most struggling children. Mary said that in this event God was remembering his promise to help Israel. As far as I was concerned, Israel stood for all who are weak, for we have been the weakest and most downtrodden of people. To be told that there is a God who cares, a God who is on the side of the oppressed, is indeed a message of hope.

  If what Mary was saying held good news for some, it held a warning for others. She said that God was putting down the mighty from their thrones. The powerful of the earth, whether individuals or nations, so often make their decisions based upon what is good for them, and they ride roughshod over the weak. They are not concerned for justice or equity or the human rights of the poor. Their time is limited. God is not in the pocket of those who wield power or sell influence.

God was scattering the proud in the imaginations of their own hearts, she said. It reminded me of the story of Babel, in which people were so confident of their technical abilities that they could do what they wanted without God. And God scattered the race because of their presumption. Every generation has the temptation of relying exclusively on its own devices. Every nation under heaven seems to be afflicted with the idea that only its welfare, only its goals are important. Those who see things that way will wind up in disarray, because it goes against the unity of the human family.

Mary went on to say that God was sending the rich away empty. The God of the universe is not impressed with wealth, she was saying. Wealth can be dangerous because it can insulate us from the problems of the poor. It hardens our hearts, makes us protective of what we have, produces selfishness rather than generosity. Mary had quite perceptively seen that such attitudes are not in keeping with the intentions of God, and that those whose eyes are blinded by wealth will eventually have that wealth removed.

That was the nature of the song she wrote. Before she left, I had her write it down for me. It is of sufficient beauty that a congregation could make it a hymn of praise. But it is also a warning to all of us of the dangers that are inherent in power, pride, and wealth.

Shortly after Mary left, Elizabeth gave birth to a son. Family members came from near and far to rejoice with us and to participate in the naming. They wanted to call him Zechariah, after me, but I took a tablet and wrote down that he was to be named John, as we had been instructed. As soon as he was named, my tongue was loosened and I was once again able to speak. Blessings and praise poured out of my mouth so abundantly that I couldn't control my tongue. A great sense of awe fell upon the people, and they began to speculate on what kind of a child John would be since so many strange things were surrounding his birth.

I was delighted to be a father, yet I could not help but think of Mary and her child, and what would become of them. If her child were to say the kinds of things about which Mary wrote, or if he were to try to make them happen, things would not go very well for him. The poor, the oppressed, the weak — they might hear him gladly. But the powerful, the wealthy, the proud — they will not hear him gladly — indeed, they will do everything they can to get rid of him. I fear for what may happen to him. On the other hand, if God really is with him, he may do great things. In any event, it is in God's hands. I just pray that whatever God asks of him, he will be faithful and able to do it.

6. Standing In Reflected Light

John 1:35-42; 6:5-9; 12:20-22

Have you ever heard someone introduced as "John, the husband of the famous Rachel So-and-So?" That can be a hard thing to live with. I know, because much of my life has been spent that way. My name is Andrew, but to most people that doesn't mean anything until I say Andrew, the brother of Simon Peter. As I said, that can be a hard thing to live with, but in my case I was given the grace to be able to accept it because of my relationship with Jesus Christ. But that gets a little ahead of my story.

My brother, Simon, and I were commercial fisherman, operating out of the village of Capernaum on the shore of the Sea of Galilee. We were in partnership with two other men, James and John, the sons of Zebedee. From time to time things were slow in our business, so when John the Baptizer came through our area I went out to listen to what he had to say. I guess you could say that I got converted by him; at least, I took my religion a lot more seriously after listening to him. I went out to be with John the Baptizer every spare moment I got. So did my fishing partner, John.

The Baptizer spoke quite a bit about someone who was to come after him, who was greater than he was. We assumed that he meant the Messiah.

One day, while we were with the Baptizer, Jesus of Nazareth, whom we knew as another itinerant preacher, passed by. When the Baptizer saw him, he said to us, "Behold the Lamb of God!" Well, that was enough to interest John and me, so we decided to follow Jesus in an effort to get better acquainted with him. I have to say right here that the Baptizer's attitude toward Jesus made quite an impression on me. He was willing to point out Jesus for us even though he could see that we might become followers of Jesus, and leave off following him. He said, "Jesus must increase, but I must decrease." You might say that the Baptizer was an example to me of a way I was later to follow.

45

Anyway, the first thing I want to tell you about is my relationship with Jesus. As I said, John and I went down the road following Jesus. We stayed a little behind him, because frankly, we didn't know what we should say if we caught up to him. Jesus must have sensed our shyness, because he stopped and asked us quite plainly, "What are you looking for?"

Now, there is a question for you; you can't get much more fundamental than that. A person can go along day by day, from one meal to the next without really asking himself, "What do I want out of life? What is my aim or my goal?" That was kind of the way I had been living life, just putting one foot in front of the other without bothering to ask whether the road I was on went where I wanted to go.

In fact, it might be a good idea for you who are listening to me to ask yourselves, "What am I looking for?" Job security perhaps? Is that possible in this changing world? Material well-being? If so, how will you know when you are well off? The opportunity to do what you are capable of doing? That's a good aim, for we all have some gift to share. How about the answer, "I am trying to learn to live as a child of God"? I like that answer. If that is *your* answer, what are you doing to discover how a child of God is supposed to live?

When John and I were presented with the question, we couldn't think of anything very important to answer, so we asked simply, "Where are you staying?" In a way it was a stall for time, for we had expected answers from this new-found teacher, and he had given us a question instead. Perhaps that, too, is important in religion: we have to have the *question* before we can know whether we have found the *answer*. Religious leaders often give answers, but they may not be answers to questions anyone is dealing with.

In addition to stalling for time, however, we really did want to know where Jesus was staying so that we could be in contact with him. If he did have answers, this fleeting conversation in the middle of a Galilean road was not going to be sufficient opportunity for us to learn from him.

Jesus' response to us was, "Come and see." At that moment we thought of it simply as an invitation to see his place of residence, but we subsequently discovered that it was an invitation to insight. Insight into what we were, what we could be, and what life could be when committed to God. These things Jesus opened up to me and I subsequently knew that I had something to share.

Therefore, the second thing I want to tell you is how following Jesus affected my relationship with my brother. Simon and I not only worked together, we were quite close to each other emotionally. Therefore, when I found something that was important to me, it was only natural that I should share it with Simon. As far as I was concerned, missionary work should begin at home. An Old Testament proverb says, "The eyes of a fool are on the ends of the earth." That means start where you are. I have since discovered that many people who are looking for something to do for Jesus will find it right in their own homes. You can't go very far toward convincing others about your faith if your life can't bear close scrutiny at home. So I told Simon, "We have found the Messiah," and I brought Simon to Jesus. You might say I was the first home missionary. I was learning to share my faith. That is something every follower of Jesus can do.

But the next lesson I had to learn was more difficult. When I introduced Jesus to Simon, Jesus said to him, "So you are Simon, the son of John? I am going to call you Peter," which means rock. Here they had just met, and it was as though Jesus knew all about Simon. He even gave Simon a nickname which suggested strength and dependability.

Thereafter, we spent a lot of time with Jesus, as much as our fishing business would allow. Eventually, Jesus asked us to give up our fishing business and to travel full time with him. It was a difficult decision, but we decided to do as Jesus asked. John and his brother, James, and others, also responded to the call.

Almost at once, Peter came to the forefront. He was often putting his foot in his mouth, but nevertheless, he was a natural leader. I guess that much of the time I was living in his shadow. Even within our small group of twelve followers there was an inner group of disciples: Peter, James, and John, who were closer to Jesus than the rest of us. They were called in when Jesus healed the daughter of a prominent man; they were present to behold the transfiguration of

Jesus; they were nearer Jesus in the agony he went through in Gethsemane. Always Peter, James, and John; seldom ever Andrew. I suppose that sometimes I resented it. After all, *I* had found Jesus first. In fact, if it weren't for me, Peter wouldn't have met Jesus at all. It is not easy when the only light that falls on you is the reflected light of a brother. But then it occurred to me that we can't all be the leader. The Baptizer's great humility in acknowledging the superior position of his cousin, Jesus, was a great lesson to me. And Jesus' suggestion that each of us was a branch of the main vine helped me to see that each of us has our own function to perform. It was not easy to be second or third or fourth, but Jesus' repeated lesson that we find greatness in service and not in position made it possible for me to avoid bitterness and to make my own unique contribution. My advice to you is that if you don't get the position you think you deserve in life, don't waste your life lamenting what you didn't get. Instead, invest your life in the opportunity you do have and God will bless your efforts.

The third thing I want to tell you about is how Jesus affected my relationship with others. First, there were the outsiders. You see, we Jews were brought up to be rather exclusive. We had so little of this world's goods that we took great pride in the distinction of being God's chosen people. We felt that God may have *created* the other peoples of the earth, but it was the Jews he *loved*. Therefore, we were exceedingly hesitant to have much to do with those who were not Jewish. We didn't eat with them, we didn't work with them, we didn't have them into our homes, and we didn't worship with them. I have known some Christians who are just about as exclusive; they won't have anything to do with people who aren't just like them. For our part, we disciples had no reason to consider non-Jews, because Jesus' ministry in Israel brought us almost exclusively into contact with Jews.

Then one day, while we were in Jerusalem, some Greeks came up to Philip and asked to see Jesus, and he in turn came to me. Here again is evidence that each of us has a unique position to play on the team. Philip and I were both from Bethsaida, a village heavily populated with Gentiles, so we had had much contact with Gentiles and were perhaps more open to them than the rest of the disciples would be. Moreover, Philip and I were the only disciples with Greek names, which may have been the reason these Greeks came to us.

I had to decide whether Jesus would be interested in speaking with Gentiles. I recalled how he frequently had good relations with the Samaritans, who at best were a mixed breed, and that one of his stories had been about a good Samaritan, so I concluded that what Jesus had to say was meant for Gentiles too. So, I brought the Gentiles to Jesus, assuming that his message was for all people. Jesus received them and indicated that all people who sought and served God would be honored by God. I learned from Jesus that there are no outsiders as far as God is concerned.

Not only did Jesus help me to become more accepting of others, he made me see that everybody has something of value to contribute. This was brought home to me that time when Jesus fed so many people. About 5,000 people had followed us to the eastern side of the Sea of Galilee to listen to Jesus. Most of them were eight to ten miles from their homes. It was late afternoon when they should have started back, but most of them had had nothing to eat during the day, and ten miles is a long walk on an empty stomach. Jesus said to Philip, "How are we going to buy bread so that these people may eat?" Philip said that we couldn't possibly afford to buy enough bread for each person to have even a taste, much less a meal. I had discovered a small boy in the crowd who still had his lunch of five small barley loaves and two fishes, which he said he was willing to share. I mentioned this to Jesus, acknowledging that it wasn't much among so many, but at least it was a beginning. Jesus agreed, gratefully accepted the boy's offer, asked God's blessing over the small portion, and we began distributing what we had to those who were there. I don't know all that happened next; maybe each person got the point and shared whatever he had been keeping for himself up to that point; maybe God just plain enlarged the elements; but everybody had enough to eat, and there was some left over. It was a profoundly moving experience. We saw one another as family.

Another point I got is that the smallest contribution is useful when turned over to God. The boy's generosity liberated the potential that was available in the crowd. And I had some part in it: I had brought the small boy to Jesus. Let no one ever despise the contribution of another as being too little; little is much when it is turned over to God.

Are you troubled by any of the things that troubled me? By slow advancement? By who gets the credit? Are you distressed because of having to remain in the background? Just look around you. There is so much to do in God's Kingdom. There are so many people who need to be brought to Jesus. Those in leadership positions can't do it all. Those in the forefront of public opinion have limited contacts. People are won to discipleship to Jesus Christ far more frequently by quiet, obscure Christians than by persons of renown. We may not be in the forefront like Peter, but each of us has something to contribute. Christ can take our little and turn it into something big. Look at what he did with five loaves and two fishes. Look at what he did with me.

7. The Doubter

John 20:19-29

My name is Thomas, but people have always called me "the twin," because I am a twin. I am one of the twelve early disciples of Jesus of Nazareth. I am certainly not the most prominent of the twelve, nor, I hope, am I the least in my contributions. I suppose that you could say that I am just about average when it comes to being a disciple. In fact, if you should ever have occasion to look up the lists of the early disciples of Jesus, you will find that I am always mentioned about half-way through. So I have no grandiose ideas about my own exalted position. But, by the same token, I feel that I can identify pretty well with a lot of other people who might classify themselves as average Christians.

What I want to say is that by the grace of God every one of us can be more than just an average Christian. And, I think that in our heart of hearts, each of us wants to be that "more." I'd like to share my own experiences of how Jesus helped me to grow, and to become that "more" of which I was capable.

One thing that I have to acknowledge is that I have always been inclined to be pessimistic. Perhaps you have heard about that time when Jesus' friend, Lazarus of Bethany, became ill. Jesus had already lost many followers because of the stringency of his requirement. Those of us who were still willing to stick by him were, at the moment, with him on the other side of the Jordan River, in Transjordan, you might say. We were there because it was just far enough away from Jerusalem to be safe. You see, Jesus had already had several encounters with the Jewish authorities in Judea, so we had spent a good deal of our time in Galilee, Samaria, and in Gentile Transjordan, just outside of their reach.

It was at that time that Jesus received word from Mary and Martha that their brother, Lazarus, was gravely ill. When Jesus heard the message, he did nothing for two days. All of us assumed

51

that was wise. If he were to cross the border and go into Bethany, he might very well encounter trouble. On the third day, however, Jesus said, "Let us go to Judea again." All of us became concerned. We said, "Rabbi, the authorities were just recently seeking to stone you. Are you sure that you want to go there again?" Jesus answered, "Our friend, Lazarus, has fallen asleep, and I need to go there to awaken him out of his sleep." Then somebody said, "Lord, if he has fallen asleep, he will be all right." Jesus then said plainly, "Lazarus is dead. For your sakes I am glad that I was not there, so that you may believe. But let us go to him."

I got the message about Lazarus being dead, but I didn't see what good Jesus could do for him now. Even so, it was obvious that Jesus was determined to go. We could hardly let him go alone. We had already shared some of the hostility that he had suffered, so I said to the other disciples, "Come on, let's all go. That way we can all die with him." That's about the way I saw that it would work out. I was pessimistic about the outcome of all of this.

Jesus, in fact, used the occasion of my pessimism to demonstrate the power of God. All of us went to Bethany. Lazarus had been dead for four days by the time we arrived. Still, Jesus went to the grave, called out Lazarus' name, and Lazarus appeared! All of us, of course, were awe-struck.

My pessimism, however, proved to be well-founded. When the authorities heard what Jesus had done, they were more determined than ever to get rid of him. Even so, if I had been pessimistic about people, I certainly had every reason to be optimistic about God. The work of Jesus plainly showed that God could and did operate in the lives of people.

Looking back, I can't say that I understood the full impact of Jesus' actions, nor did I understand the full extent of his powers, but he certainly redeemed me from having a totally pessimistic attitude about life. I felt that death would no longer be a problem for us. I suspect that was a part of what Jesus wanted us to feel — that death should not be a problem — but at that time, I felt there would be no death at all — and in that I was being unrealistic. Still, Jesus had redeemed me from pessimism.

Another thing Jesus did for me: he helped me to understand God better. Not long after the raising of Lazarus, we all went up to Jerusalem to celebrate the Passover. On the night of the Passover meal, we were together in an upper room. Jesus did a strange thing: he took a basin of water and a towel and began to wash our feet. When some of us protested, he pointed out that this was to demonstrate that each of us was called to serve. I could understand that; his words were plain. Then he spoke of someone betraying him, and of Peter denying him. That part was vague to me.

Finally, he said that he was going away. That was news to me. I was glad when Peter asked him, "Where are you going?" but I didn't understand the answer. Jesus spoke of going to the Father's house and of preparing a place for us. He said, "Where I am going you know, and the way you know." After that no one asked him anything further about it. It was as if they were all satisfied with the answer, and I was the only one who didn't understand. So I pressed the point and said, "Lord, we don't know where you are going. How can we know the way?" I was asking that question for myself, to be sure, but as I look back, I think that it was a question that anyone might ask, even today.

Jesus took the occasion of my question to bring out one of his most important lessons. He said, "I am the way, and the truth, and the life. No one comes to the Father except through me." Jesus was saying that he was the way to God. If we wanted to find God, it would be through him, his way, his teaching. He went on to say that he and the Father were one, meaning that whoever had seen Jesus had seen God. I had not thought of him in that way before. Oh, I had recognized something unique in him. I thought of him as a prophet, a teacher — yes, even as the Messiah. But now he was saying that God himself could be seen in him. Jesus had taken me, an average person, without much theological background, and had made it possible for me to experience God. I was no longer ignorant; I had seen the truth.

The next experience I want to share with you is how Jesus overcame my disillusionment. I suppose that this is the experience that people most often think about when they hear about me. I think that it is particularly significant for anyone who is troubled by questions and doubts about Jesus.

Following that wonderful experience in the upper room that night, we disciples accompanied Jesus to the Garden of Gethsemane for rest and prayer. Each of us, I think, felt that the glorious revelation of Jesus' power was imminent. But before the night was over, Jesus was betrayed, led away, and imprisoned without a fight. The next day I saw him tried, beaten, crucified, killed, and buried. This was God? This was the one who raised someone else from the dead? I fled in terror and disappointment, utterly disillusioned.

The other disciples had somehow managed to stay together, more out of fear than loyalty, I think. Several days after the crucifixion they were all together in one place, behind locked doors. I was not there; I had quit their number. That night Jesus appeared to them. There was no question about it, they said. He came among them, showed them his hands and side, breathed his spirit upon them, and said, "Peace be with you."

When I saw them several days later, they told me about it. I thought that they had had an hallucination. Or perhaps they were just trying to cheer me up. Frankly, I was surprised to hear that they were still meeting together. Didn't they realize that it was over? I said, "Unless I see in his hands the mark of the nails, and place my finger in the mark of the nails, and place my hand in his side, I will not believe." There was, after all, a limit to my credulity. I wanted tangible evidence.

I was much in thought during the next several days, however. The others seemed so certain. Perhaps I had made a mistake in isolating myself from the group as I had. It began to occur to me that when we are troubled by doubt or sorrow, we need the fellowship of other Christians even more than when our faith is strong. For my part, I missed an experience with Christ that I desperately needed because I had cut myself off from the fellowship. When we are alone, we miss things that can only be experienced with others. If I were to give any advice to you based on what I learned from my experience, it would be that when you are going through a time of trial in your faith, stay closer than ever to the community of faith. Don't feel that you have to be such a confident believer to be a part of the fellowship. As I came to this conclusion, I once again joined in the gathering of the fellowship.

On the next Sunday, we were all together in the same place again, behind locked doors, and Jesus came and stood among us. Again he said, "Peace be with you." Then he looked at me and said, "Put your finger here, Thomas, and feel my hands; and put out your hand, and place it in my side. Do not doubt, Thomas, but believe." I didn't need to touch him. I fell to my knees in reverence, saying, "My Lord and my God." He had come to me in my weakness to give me strength. He had not required a certain level of commitment from me first, only an openness so that I could be approached. He accepted me as I was, with my doubts and misgivings, and he ministered to my need. My friends, you do not have to have everything solved before you can call yourself a follower of Jesus Christ. I am confident from my experience that if you only honestly seek him, he will make himself known to you. He helped me overcome my doubt.

Let me share one last experience I had with the risen Lord. By now I had become a convinced believer. I was once again in close association with the other disciples. But there our understanding ended. We had returned to Galilee and gone back to fishing. We still had faith, but no direction. One morning, after fishing all night and catching nothing, while we were still out on the Sea of Galilee, some distance from the shore, someone on the shore called to us and asked whether we had caught anything. We replied, "No," whereupon the person on the shore said, "Cast the net to the right side of the boat and you will find fish." We tried it, and made a great catch. John strained his eyes to see who was giving us this advice, and declared, "It is the Lord!" Upon hearing that, Peter jumped into the water and swam ashore. It was, in fact, Jesus on the shore. He talked with us and shared a meal with us as he had done on so many occasions.

It was not the great draft of fish that impressed us. It was the awareness that when we were operating on our own we were not succeeding, but that when we were under the direction of Jesus we were successful. I don't mean to apply this in some crass business sense, as though to say that if we had kept at fishing, Jesus would have guaranteed our wealth. He was teaching us that if we submitted our lives to his direction, he would use us to bring about results. Each of us got the message and submitted ourselves to be instruments open to his direction. From that moment, we have been partners with Jesus Christ.

He led me from pessimism about people to optimism about God, from ignorance of God's nature to understanding God as Father, from disillusionment to faith, from unrewarding enterprise to purposeful living. I, Thomas the doubter, became Thomas the dedicated disciple through the grace and help of Jesus Christ. That same path is open to you!

8. All Things To All People

1 Corinthians 9:16-23

I was raised to believe that if you did what you believed to be right, God would bless you by making your life easier because the light of his favor would shine on you. I have come to recognize that is not necessarily true. You may be happier, you may be more fulfilled, you may be more certain about the outcome of life; but life will not necessarily be easier. Look at Jesus. If anyone ever lived God's way, he did. And he died on a cross. The world is still in the process of being saved, and when we enlist in that process, it will undoubtedly cost us something, too.

Pardon me, I hadn't intended to get into preaching. At least, not quite so soon. My name is Paul, called to be an apostle of Jesus Christ, and I have a story to tell which I think supports the point I was just trying to make. I think God has called each of us to serve him, and we are expected to do that, whatever it costs. My own story unfolds in various geographical settings, and I will refer to those as I share my experiences.

I was born in Tarsus, an important cultural city of Asia Minor, about ten years after the birth of Christ. The city was Greek-speaking, and quite cosmopolitan. Although my family heritage was Jewish, my father was a Roman citizen, and I became one at birth. We belonged to the strictest party of Judaism, the Pharisees. Being born in Tarsus made me open to the Gentile world in ways that would not have been possible if I had been born in Palestine. It also meant that I would learn the language of Western culture, Greek. I did not know it then, but these characteristics were going to become very valuable to me later.

The next geographical area to make an impact upon me was Jerusalem. From an early age it had been decided that I would become a rabbi, so when I became old enough, I was sent to Jerusalem to study the Jewish law with the great scholar, Gamaliel. I also learned a trade. I became a tentmaker, for it was felt that a rabbi should be able to support himself. As a Pharisee I became more and more convinced that the heart of true religion was a meticulous performance of ritual. We Pharisees focused on fulfilling the ceremonial law as the way to get right with God.

While I was a student, I became aware of a sect within Judaism that called itself the Way. Its leader, Jesus, had been crucified some years before I arrived in Jerusalem. Its adherents discounted portions of the ceremonial law and claimed that Jesus was the long-awaited Jewish Messiah. I felt that they needed to be rooted out, lest they lead others astray. I saw to it that one of their number, a man by the name of Stephen, was brought to trial and stoned to death. I asked for, and then received, letters from the religious authorities to go where I could to find these followers of the Way and bring them to Jerusalem for trial.

So it was that I set out for Damascus as a true believer in what I was doing. Yet, I couldn't get over the way Stephen had died for what he believed to be the truth. Moreover, it impressed me that he died, not cursing those who were killing him, but asking God to forgive us. About noon on the second day of our journey to Damascus, I was struck by a bright light that knocked me to the ground. Then I heard a voice that said, "Saul! Saul! Why do you persecute me?" I was dazed and blinded by what happened. Call it sunstroke, call it a seizure; whatever it was, God used it to get through to me. I was led into Damascus by others, and I remained blind for several days, until a Christian man by the name of Ananias came, placed his hands on me, and healed me. The blindness was a frightening experience. I think that it symbolized my spiritual blindness up to that point. When the blindness left, I was suddenly ready to follow Jesus, and I began to preach about him in the synagogue. When the Jewish leaders heard this, they were enraged and watched the gates, seeking to kill me as a traitor and heretic. I escaped with my life because some of the followers of Jesus let me down from the city walls by basket at night so I could escape. I fled to the desert and spent some time there, sorting through my experience.

I went back to Damascus some time later, but the Jewish leaders were still hostile, so I decided to return to Jerusalem to talk with the leaders of the church. At first they didn't want to see me, because they thought my change of mind was only a ruse to entrap them and arrest them. Actually, I think the leaders of the church were anxious to send me away because I was the cause of dissension with the Jews.

I returned to Tarsus, preached the Good News of God's love for all people as best I could, supported myself as a tentmaker, and spent the next ten years forgotten by the church. Toward the end of that time, some Jewish followers of Jesus in Antioch, Syria, began to tell certain Gentiles, that is non-Jews, about their faith. When the Gentiles became interested and wanted to become believers, the church leaders in Jerusalem sent one of their own, a man named Barnabas, to find out what was going on. Barnabas got into the spirit of what they were doing and began to have great success winning Gentiles to Jesus. He then remembered me, came to visit me in Tarsus, and invited me to come and help him in the church at Antioch. I jumped at the chance, and we worked together for a year in Antioch. We kept in contact with the Jews in the synagogue at Antioch, but our work went so much better among the non-Jews that we tended to see the Way as less and less a sect within Judaism and more and more a separate movement.

We were anxious to test elsewhere what we were discovering in Antioch, so we asked the church there to send us out on a mission. Little did we know that this was going to be the method God was going to honor for the expansion of his church. We started with the island of Cyprus, as that was Barnabas' home, and he was in charge. John Mark, a cousin of Barnabas, accompanied us. It was there that I decided to change my Hebrew name, Saul, to the Greek name, Paul, and so identify myself with the Greek culture we were entering.

We sailed for Asia Minor, and when we arrived, I became so ill I almost died. John Mark became discouraged and left us. When I regained a little strength, we pressed forward into Galatia, preaching in a number of cities, always starting with a synagogue if one existed. When the Jews rejected our testimony, as they usually did, we turned to the Gentiles and met with success. The Jews would then become angry and threaten to stone us, so we would have to leave, but a small church would be established. When we were at Lystra, some Jews came from another city and stirred up some of the townspeople against us. We were dragged out of town, stoned, and left for dead. However, our Christian friends revived us, cared for us, and sent us on our way. Do not think ill of my Jewish brothers and sisters for such things. I myself had been as they in my blind rage. They were simply afraid that something very precious to them was being profaned by being offered to non-Jews. They could not see what we were coming to realize: that God loves *all* people, and that he had sent Jesus to proclaim that fact.

After spending some months establishing half a dozen churches in Asia Minor, we decided to retrace our steps, strengthening the churches, and making our way back to Antioch. Barnabas and I settled down to work once again among the Gentile believers in Antioch. About that time, some Jewish Christians from Jerusalem arrived and circulated the idea that what we were doing was not right: they insisted that Gentile Christians must be circumcised, and essentially become Jews, in order to be proper Christians.

Barnabas and I went at once to Jerusalem to discuss the matter with the church leaders. The church leaders agreed with our point of view. They gave us their blessing to go and work among Gentiles, and they pledged their cooperation. The only thing they asked was that we try to raise money for the poor of Jerusalem, where the situation was very bad economically. I thought the issue was resolved, but I was badly mistaken. There seems to be an exclusive attitude in human beings that seeks to set up limitations and to exclude other people from the faith, rather than to include them.

Barnabas and I returned to Antioch, but we couldn't help wondering how our new churches in Asia Minor were doing. I proposed to him that we go to visit them. He agreed, but he wanted to take John Mark again. I refused, for Mark had left us before when the going got tough. When Barnabas insisted on taking John Mark, I suggested that we divide the work. He and John Mark should go to Cyprus, since that was Barnabas' country, and I would take another fellow, named Silas, and visit the churches of Asia Minor. Barnabas agreed. Silas and I set out for Asia Minor, where we visited each of the churches that Barnabas and I had established. All were doing well and greeted us hospitably.

We felt, however, that the rest of Asia Minor was being closed to us for the moment. We felt that God had something else for us to do. So it was that we made our way to Troas, near ancient Troy, on the Aegean Sea. It was there that we met Luke, a Gentile physician from Philippi in Macedonia. He joined our group and began to tell us about life in Europe. One night I had a vision in which a man dressed as a Macedonian stood before me and said, "Come over to Macedonia and help us." I was convinced that we had received our next assignment.

We crossed over to Macedonia, began preaching in Philippi, and met with some success. We traveled through Macedonia and on into Greece, visiting principal cities and establishing churches. Always our pattern was to begin, when we could, in the synagogue. Sometimes the Jews would hear us gladly, but when our work prospered, some of them would become jealous of our success, start a riot, force us out of town, and even follow us to the next place, where they would create more turmoil for us.

It had now been almost three years since we had left Antioch, and I felt the need to return and report on what we had been doing, so we returned to Antioch and made our report.

Shortly thereafter we began to receive messages that many of the churches we had established were in need of more strengthening. So, as soon as I could, I set out on yet another journey to visit and to strengthen the churches.

I visited the churches in Asia Minor and moved on to Ephesus on the Aegean. Other Christians, Timothy, Titus, Erastus, and others, became my associates in proclaiming the gospel. I labored there for two years, and the church grew to such proportions that we had to hire a lecture hall. One day a riot broke out in Ephesus because our proclamation that there is one God was having an adverse effect on the silversmiths, who made images of the patron deity of Ephesus, Diana. Again, we were forced to leave town.

I was now looking westward to Rome and beyond that to Spain. I wanted desperately to go to Rome, where there was already a church, but I felt obliged to take the offering from the Gentile churches to Jerusalem. Someone else might have done this, but I felt that I needed to interpret the significance of an offering from Gentile Christians to meet the needs of poor Jewish Christians in Jerusalem. So I wrote a letter to the Christians in Rome, telling them that I hoped to come their way soon, but that, for the moment, I could not come.

We set out for Jerusalem by ship, stopping periodically along the way, finding fellowship with Christian churches. Everywhere we stopped, Christian people warned me of how dangerous it was for me to go to Jerusalem. I knew that was the case, and I began to have premonitions that if I went there, it would somehow be the end for me. Yet, I could not put it off. I had to go.

When we arrived in Jerusalem, it was a tense city. We found unrest, distrust, false messiahs leading the people astray, Roman executions, and Jewish terrorist squads. The Jerusalem Christians were glad to see us and to hear of our experiences during the past few years. However, they were still concerned to keep up their contacts with Judaism, for many Jewish Christians still felt that Christianity was a part of Judaism. They urged me to show that, whatever else I might be, I was still a good Jew. They urged me to do what I could to overcome some of the apprehensions some Christian Jews had about me.

They suggested that I accompany a group of Jewish young men who were going to the temple to perform a ritual in fulfillment of a vow. I wanted desperately to keep the Gentile and Jewish wings of the church together, so I consented. Over and over I have been prepared to be all things to all people if it would help to get the gospel across. To the poor, I became poor; to the Gentiles, I became as one of them. Therefore, I could accommodate to Jewish sensitivities also, so long as it wasn't a requirement being placed on Gentiles. While I was in the temple area, some Jews who knew me from Ephesus happened to come into the temple compound. They saw the four young men, assumed that they were Gentiles, and were convinced that I was defiling the temple. A riot ensued, in which they would have pulled me limb from limb had not a Roman colonel and a squad of Roman soldiers come to my rescue. I was taken off to prison for my own safety.

At that moment, over such a seemingly minor matter, my liberty came to an end. I have not been really free since. The next day I was brought before the Jewish Council so that they might formalize charges, but they could not agree on the charges. That night as I was trying to sleep, I saw a vision of Christ standing at my side and saying: "Courage! For just as you have testified for me in Jerusalem, you must testify in Rome also." So I was going to get to go to Rome after all! Not in the manner I had expected, but I would get there.

That night, for my safety, I was transferred to the Roman capital of Palestine, at Caesarea. The Roman governor, Felix, tried to determine the charges, but he was not able to get a clear picture of the problem. I was kept in confinement for two years. Periodically, Felix would have me brought to him, and I was able to tell him about the Lord Jesus. But he did not believe. When Felix was recalled to Rome, a new governor was appointed. He wanted to send me to Jerusalem for trial, but I knew that would be a death sentence, so I appealed to be sent to Rome to be tried by Caesar, which was my right as a Roman citizen.

It was a poor time for a voyage. It was getting into late fall. I was part of a contingent of prisoners to be sent to Rome under the guard of a Roman captain and his men. Two of my friends were able to accompany me. We were caught in a terrible storm, and eventually shipwrecked on the island of Malta, where we were obliged to spend the winter. In the spring we took ship once again, and eventually arrived in Italy. News of my coming had been carried to the Christian churches so that all the way to Rome, Christians came out and accompanied us in procession.

I have been living in Rome for two years now, under a kind of house arrest. People are able to come and see me, and in my confinement I am able to preach and also to write to the congregations where I have preached. The Christians at Philippi are contributing to my living expenses. My case has not come to trial, because all the papers regarding my case were lost in the shipwreck. I feel that the trial is getting closer, however, and I am not optimistic about the outcome, for the emperor, Nero, is not kindly disposed toward anything that contributes to disturbance.

I am now at the point of being sacrificed; the time of my departure is at hand. I have fought the good fight, I have finished the race, I have kept the faith. That is what I wanted to accomplish by telling you my story. Following Jesus is often not easy, as you have heard from my story, but it is, nevertheless, the most fulfilling life I know. I would not have traded it for anything.

When you are called to go through tough times, do not give up. Hold fast to Jesus Christ, and he will give you the courage to do what you need to do.

9. The Lepers' Friend

John 15:12-17

When I was a child, we used to ice skate for hours in the winter on the canals near my home. I never dreamed there was a place without snow. I have not seen snow for 25 years, and trying to explain it to people who live on this tropical island is quite a challenge. I have not seen a member of my family for 25 years either, but then, I guess you could say that my family is really right here with me on this island. These people, among whom I now live, are my brothers and sisters and children.

My name is Damien — Father Damien. Actually, my parents named me Joseph — Joseph De Veuster — after Saint Joseph, the carpenter. I was born in Tremelo, Belgium, in 1840. My father was a farmer and grain merchant. He wanted me to go into the grain business, too. Our required schooling ended at age thirteen, and at that age I began to work for my father. After several years, it became apparent that, to be in business, I needed to know French, so, at the age of seventeen, I was sent to boarding school to learn French. It was while I was away from home that I felt the call to the religious life. My brother, Pamphile, had already become a priest, and a sister had become a nun. My parents felt they had already done their part for the church, but they did not try to dissuade me.

I wrote to my brother, who was part of an order called the Congregation of Sacred Hearts, and told him of my decision. He urged me to join him. I was received into the order as a lay brother in 1859, and I was given the religious name of Damien — Brother Damien. Soon, thereafter, I decided to study for the priesthood, though studies never came easily to me, and I had considerable catching up to do.

Several years later, my brother was chosen to go as a missionary to what we called the Sandwich Islands — better knows as the Hawaiian Islands. Shortly before the date of his departure, he contracted typhoid and was not going to be able to go. I volunteered in his place and, though I was not yet a priest, I was accepted. Seventeen of us — one priest, three future priests, three lay brothers, and ten nuns — set sail from Bremerhaven in October, 1863. We arrived in Honolulu 140 days later, in March, 1864.

Hawaii was a strange place for Belgian Catholics to be serving. The Islands had been united by a chieftain between 1784 and 1810, and turned into a kingdom. Protestants had been the first to come as missionaries and were well received by the natives. In fact, for many years, the Protestants had used their initial influence to keep Catholic missionaries out. In 1839, a French frigate trained its guns on Honolulu and threatened to bombard the city if Roman Catholic priests were not allowed to land and establish churches. Under such inauspicious beginnings, Catholic work began in the Islands, and grew rapidly.

When I arrived, the bishop to whom I was assigned sent me to school in order to complete my theological studies and to learn Kanaka, the Hawaiian language. I was ordained a priest several months later and assigned to a section of the island of Hawaii. I had a huge parish. It took me six weeks to make my rounds. We had no churches, so mass was offered in the huts of the people. Eventually, the natives and I built a little church. We had no bell, so people were called to Mass by someone blowing on a conch shell. How I loved those people! I worked there seven years — and we built a chapel a year. My parents rightly named me Joseph, after the carpenter, for much of my time and energy were spent in building churches.

The subject I really want to talk about was developing even before I arrived. In 1863, concern had been expressed publicly over the increase of leprosy in the Islands. Two years later, the king decreed that a place should be found in the Islands where lepers could be isolated. The island of Molokai was chosen, and a board of health was set up in Honolulu to enforce the exile of lepers and to administer the colony. Of course, lepers resisted going into exile, but by 1866, 140 lepers had been sent to Molokai. They were simply dropped off on a beach and required to walk to the so-called hospital — a large, barn-like structure with no beds, no nurses, and no doctors. The worst cases just stayed there, unbandaged and unwashed, until they died.

The board of health had thought that, with a little outside help, the lepers would form a self-sustaining colony. Instead, the lepers felt that they had been sentenced to a penal colony from which there was no parole. Old residents took advantage of new ones, and announced, "Here there is no law." Days and nights were spent in sleeping, gambling, drinking, and orgies. Children were even forced into prostitution. On that unfortunate island, chaos reigned.

Some years later, a new board of health was created. An attempt was made to improve the supply of rations sent to the island. The king publicly expressed concern for the well-being of his subjects. A journalist wrote in a newspaper: "Anyone who would consent to go to the aid of these unhappy people would deserve the blessings of all mankind. Is there nowhere a priest inspired to go and live among them, and sacrifice his life for them?" At that time, it was the practice of our church for a priest to go and spend several days there in a year. The Catholic lepers were pleading for a more frequent priest who might, at least, bring about the salvation of their souls.

The bishop asked for volunteers who would be willing to go and serve for three months at a time. I volunteered at once, for I felt that was where God wanted me. And I knew from the outset that it would not be a three-month stay, for I had seen parishioners with the disease, and I knew that the assignment would have to be for life.

I arrived on Molokai in May, 1873. The bishop accompanied me, and he spoke to the lepers saying: "Hitherto you have been alone and abandoned, but all that is over and done with. This good Father has come to be with you. We shall never abandon you, neither while you live, nor when you die." There was not even a place for me to stay when I arrived, so I slept under a tree until lumber arrived which enabled me to build a small hut, ten by sixteen feet. I was, of course, daily surrounded by the lepers. I visited them in their huts and was frequently offered poi, into which I would be obliged to dip a finger or two. Leprosy is a most dreadful disease! It eats away the flesh, and as the flesh rots it gives off a horrible odor. Yet God gave me strength to visit these people in their huts, to offer extreme unction to the dying, to hear confession, and to offer mass.

When I arrived, there was a collection of brush huts housing about 800 lepers. There was not a doctor in the place, but as there was no cure for the disease, a doctor's skills were of no use anyway. Any doctoring was done by a white man, who was a leper, and myself. Each day, after Mass, I would visit the sick, about half of whom were Catholic. Most, even non-Catholics, regarded me as a father. I identified myself with the real lepers in order to win all for Christ. That is why, when I preached, I would say, "We lepers," not "My brothers and sisters."

By the time I had been there six months, I had baptized more than a hundred persons, and buried as many, for someone died nearly every day. There was no money for funeral expenses, so we buried people in blankets. Whenever I had the opportunity, I would make a coffin. In fact, in the sixteen years I have served on this island, I have buried 1,800 of my people — and I made coffins for more than a thousand of them. I did what I could to minister to their spiritual and physical needs, washing and bandaging sores and offering words of comfort. I confess that I often wept when I was alone, for from morning to night, I was in the midst of such bodily and spiritual wretchedness that my heart could break. Yet, I forced myself always to be cheerful in order to give some courage to my unhappy sufferers.

I soon realized that visitation would not be enough. The lepers lived in brush huts, which were dark and usually wet, because they did not keep out the rain. A year after I arrived, most of these huts were destroyed by a hurricane. I appealed to the superintendent, who lived on another part of the island, separated from the leper colony, to supply us with lumber. This he did, and in time we built permanent wooden huts, and gave them all a coat of whitewash. Once again, whatever carpentry skills I had picked up on my father's farm were put to use.

There was also a problem with the water supply. Drinking water had to be carried from a stream, which was a long way from the homes of the lepers. Some were too ill to make the journey and had to rely on what their neighbors could spare. I appealed to the superintendent for water pipe, and he saw to it that we got it, but we had to engineer it and lay it ourselves. Nevertheless, we succeeded in bringing water from the interior of the island into the settlement, even managing to ensure that there was a tap near every hut.

In time, our little settlement turned into a village with white-washed huts, a church, flower beds, and patches of vegetables. I tried to get every leper capable of working to do so. Eventually, we had more than enough vegetables for ourselves, and we even managed to sell some, so that the lepers could make a little money. The work was good therapy and helped them overcome their frequent depression. I opened a small store where they could use their money, and most of them were proud to be able to earn money and to pay for their goods.

The Hawaiians are a very musical people, and in time we were able to use this talent to help overcome depression. At first, we started out with improvised instruments, but eventually people sent instruments from Honolulu. We developed a small musical group and a choir. Due to the disease, there was a continuous turnover in the membership of the musical groups. We had several funerals a week, and these were always accompanied by our colorful band.

Our church was the significant center of everything. After I had been there a few years, we would have 300 to 400 present for Sunday Mass. Though 100 or 200 persons might die in a year, the population of lepers always remained at about 700. We developed confraternities in the church — what you might call societies. There was one for those who adored the sacrament: people devoted to the veneration of Christ. There was the confraternity of Holy Child-hood for those concerned with babies and youngsters. The confra-ternity of Saint Joseph was our men's group, and the confraternity of the Blessed Virgin was dedicated to meeting the needs of women lepers. Whenever we would meet as a congregation, people wore brightly colored sashes to indicate the confraternity to which they belonged.

At night many would come and gather around my hut and tell me of their Hawaiian legends. Then they would listen while I told them stories of Belgium. Though I was consumed with my work day and night, I loved my lepers, and nothing could make me leave them. They also loved me, and some said they would not leave the island, even if they could, if it meant leaving me behind.

The board of health was apparently satisfied with what was happening, too. They offered me $10,000 a year if I would accept the position of deputy superintendent. That was a considerable salary in 1877. I told them: "I would not stay here five minutes for $100,000. Love of God, and love for these people are the only reasons why I remain. If I were to accept salary for my work, my mother would no longer own me as her son."

In 1881, Princess Liliuokalani, acting as Regent for her brother, the King, paid us a visit. She was to address the lepers, but she was too overcome by what she saw and could not speak. The Prime Minister spoke instead. Subsequently, she knighted me, and made me a Commander of the Royal Order of Kalakaua. I still have the insignia, and I wear it on certain national holidays, but it tends to make my old priestly robe look even more shabby than it is. I did not care much for the publicity, but the newsmen were very kind, and the news of our work, carried around the world, did bring in funds with which we could help the lepers. All in all, it has been very gratifying to be here and to do something worthwhile.

Then, inevitably, there came the discovery that I, too, had the disease. I suppose that I never doubted that one day I would contract it. I had been experiencing some symptoms for years, but as often as not, they would go away. I became absolutely sure on an evening in December, 1884. I had been out making rounds in the huts of the lepers until quite late that evening. I was cold, and I decided to soak my feet in hot water before I went to bed. I didn't pay too much attention to what I was doing, and I filled the bowl with boiling water instead of hot water. When I put my feet in the water, I saw them turn scarlet, I pulled them out and watched the blisters appear, but I felt no pain. That's when I knew — knew without any shadow of doubt — that I, too, was a leper, for one of the sure signs of leprosy is that parts of the body become insensible to pain.

When a doctor made a brief visit to the Island, he examined me, and confirmed that I had the disease. I wrote to my Superior General and told him, "One of your spiritual children has been decorated, not only with the royal Cross of Kalakaua, but also with the cross of leprosy, which is a trifle heavier to bear." In spite of this setback, God has given me the strength to continue to function. In fact, I would refuse to be cured if the price of it had to be my departure from the Island and the abandonment of all my work here. No doubt I contributed to my getting the disease by my close contact with the lepers — touching them, going into their huts, wrapping their sores, feeding them, and working with them. For I have determined to do nothing that would make the lepers feel unclean or rejected. So, I have been reckless. I have preferred love to caution. I became a fool for the sake of Christ.

My reason for telling you all this is not to acquaint you with what we have done in this leper colony, but to remind you that individuals count. There is power in this world that doesn't lie with the big battalions. An individual, like myself, not endowed with any special gifts, can accomplish great things for God and others. Very ordinary people, who love God and love God's children, can count for something when they are willing to put love into action. That kind of love is dangerous, but it is also exciting, for it brings with it the sense of having participated in something worthwhile. I urge each of you to find your own Molokai, and when you do, transform it into a garden of love. And if it is costly, remember the words of our Lord: "Greater love has no one than this — that one lay down one's life for a friend."

10. Never On Sunday

Hebrews 11:32—12:2

I've experienced some paralysis in my left leg in recent days, some halting in my speech, and there are these recurring headaches. It is not like me. I've always been so healthy, so filled with energy. Those who have examined me say it is probably exhaustion. I've been trying to do too much in our effort to turn this prison compound into some sort of community. What keeps me going is the thought that my wife Florence, my daughters Patricia, Heather, and little Maureen, whom I have never seen, are safe in Canada. And the Lord has been with me. Indeed, I have often claimed for myself that verse in Isaiah that says, "... they that wait upon the Lord shall renew their strength, they shall mount up with wings like eagles, they shall run and not be weary, they shall walk and not faint." To run and not be weary. That has often been my experience. When I have run I have felt God's pleasure.

My name is Eric Liddell. If you follow track at all, you may have heard about me. God gave me the ability to run, and that ability, in turn, helped me to touch the lives of others for Christ. Running has little to do with why you find me here now, in a Japanese internment camp, but all my experiences are related to my desire to serve God. If you have the time, I'd like to tell you about it.

My parents, who originated in Scotland, were both Congregational missionaries, serving in China. They came out here in 1899. Just about that time nationalistic Chinese, known as Boxers, were calling on peasants to drive all foreigners, especially Christians, from China. Before the Boxers were put down by the European powers, 200 Western missionaries and 30,000 Chinese Christians had been killed.

My parents had been serving in Mongolia, but had to flee to Tientsin where my brother, Robert, was born in 1900. Two years later I was born. My sister, Jenny, and brother, Ernest, were also born in China. In 1907 we returned to Scotland for a furlough. When my parents returned to China, in 1908, it was decided that Robert and I should stay in a boarding school for missionary children in Scotland. I was competent in my studies, but over the years I excelled in athletics — cricket, rugby, and especially, track.

In 1920, I graduated from the boarding school and entered the University of Edinburgh for a four-year course in science. A friend heard that I had done some running in boarding school and encouraged me to go out for track at the University. I did, and raced against the school favorite. I lost by inches in the 220-yard race. It was the last race I would lose in Scotland. I began training in earnest. In 1922, I won the Scottish championships in the 100-yard and 220-yard events. In 1923, I broke the records for the 100, 220, and 440. Every week I was privileged to bring home new trophies for the school. I do not say these things to boast. I am convinced that the ability to accomplish these things came from God.

In 1923, a friend asked me to speak at a Christian Evangelistic meeting. I had been a Christian as far back as I could remember — we were rooted in an evangelical fundamentalist tradition — but I had never given a public testimony. On that occasion, I declared my faith in Christ before about eighty young men. I have never been much of a public speaker, but people were interested in listening because of my track record, and so I was invited to speak often, especially before groups of students and young adults.

The time for the 1924 Olympic Games, to be held in Paris, was approaching. In 1923, at a triangular contest between England, Scotland, and Ireland, I won the 100, the 220, and the 440, but I had what others called an appalling running style: head back, making it difficult to see the track, arms pummeling the air. I never should have won anything. When asked what was the secret of my success in the 440, I responded: "In the first half I run as fast as I can, and the second half I run faster with God's help." People expected me to give a more pious reason, like prayer. I told them simply, "The fact is, I don't like to be beaten." I was chosen to run the 100-meter and the 200-meter races for Britain in the Olympic Games. The 100-meter was the jewel of the Games, and I wanted sorely to win it. Then the timetables came out. The heats for the

100-meter were to be held on a Sunday. All my life I had been taught that Sunday was the Lord's Day. For me it was the Sabbath. It was a day for worship and prayer, not for competition.

I said I would not run on a Sunday. The British athletic authorities were horrified. Some newspapers called me a traitor. The 100-meter and 400-meter relays were also scheduled for a Sunday. I had to bow out of those. The athletic authorities then asked me to train for the 400-meter race. I began the arduous training for that event and discovered that I was well suited to it.

It was an unusually hot July in Paris that year, up to 113 degrees. Long-distance runners were dropping like flies. Even as we prepared for the races, my teammates kept urging me to compete in the other races. I felt I was letting my country down, but on Sunday, July 6, as others were running, I was off preaching at a small Scots church in Paris. On July 7, Harold Abrahams, a fellow Britisher, won the 100 meter. He went on to serve in athletics for the rest of his life. On July 8, I won the bronze in the 200 meter, but it was hardly noted in the Scots press. On July 10, I successfully survived the various rounds of the 400 meter, and in the finals I won the gold in world record time. The Scots press went wild.

My return to Scotland the following week coincided with my graduation from the University. Those planning the event presented me with an olive wreath and a poem written in my honor. Students carried me in a sedan chair to St. Giles Church, where there were more speeches. I reminded the students that we humans are composed of body, mind, and spirit, and only when each part is nurtured will we have the truest harmony for which God made us. At a dinner the next day I announced that running was not to be my career. My parents and my sister were serving as missionaries in China; my brother, Rob, had gone back as a medical missionary; and I intended to be a missionary also. There had been no dramatic moment of decision. I had always known that this is what I would do.

I subsequently enrolled at Scottish Congregational College so I could satisfy some of the theological requirements of my missionary service. I continued to run in some events, and I did well, but most of my spare time was spent in evangelistic work among the young men of Scotland. I don't have a great oratory style, but people came to hear me anyway, because of my accomplishment. In the summer of 1925 a great crowd came to the Edinburgh Railroad Station to see me off. Someone started to sing "Jesus Shall Reign," and soon all the station was belting out hymn after hymn.

When I arrived in China that summer, the Chinese were seething under foreign exploitation and unfair treaties. I was to teach science and supervise athletics and religious work at the Anglo-Chinese College in Tientsin. The Chinese were living in wretched poverty, while Europeans and Japanese lived safely in national neighborhoods with their own armies, police forces, and laws. The Chinese tolerated foreigners, but didn't like them. Missionaries were seen as symbols of western imperialism, and Chinese Christians were seen as lackeys. Control of the country was in the hands of hundreds of warlords. The Nationalists and the Communists were vying for power. China was a powder keg, ready to explode.

I continued to run, mostly against foreign troops stationed in China. Once I was in a race in Darien, Japan. There were just twenty minutes between the end of the race and the departure of the boat for my return to China. I won the race and kept on going, but the band started to play "God Save The King" and the "Marseillaise," so I had to stop and stand at attention. I hopped into a taxi and arrived at the dock as the boat was pulling out. I made a flying fifteen-foot jump and landed on the deck of the boat.

Among my duties in China was the superintendency of the Sunday school at the Union Church. Playing the piano there was Florence McKenzie, the daughter of Canadian missionaries. I fell in love with her and proposed to her in 1930. She accepted, but indicated that she needed to return to Canada for training as a nurse. That postponed our marriage for four years. I visited her and her family in Canada, as well as my own parents in Edinburgh, who were by then retired, when I was on furlough in 1931. The purpose of my furlough was to complete the course of study that would lead to my ordination. That was accomplished in 1932. While I was in Scotland, a reporter asked if I missed running, if I was sorry I had given up the competition. I responded, "A fellow's life counts for far more in what I am doing now than in running." The joy of breaking the tape, of being good at something brings satisfaction, but surrender to God means more.

While I was away from China, Japan invaded Manchuria in 1931. When I returned, a vicious civil war was under way between the Communist Red Army and the Nationalists. Florence completed her training and returned to Tientsin in 1934. We were married in March. During the next several years our two oldest daughters were born. I relished being with them and watching them grow. However, drought and the civil war were causing the mission board to seek missionaries who would work in the devastated villages of the interior. I did not want to leave my family, but I felt obliged to go.

I went to Siaochang, an impoverished village, caught between Japanese soldiers, Chinese guerrillas, and wandering bandits. Our mission compound, surrounded by mud walls, housed a hospital and a girls' school. I was an itinerating evangelist, visiting churches in an area the size of Wales. The people were suffering great privation, taxation, poor crops, and violence from all sides. Yet they were willing to hear the gospel. Executions were common. We collected the wounded and brought them to our hospital. I would periodically return to Tientsin to visit my family.

Eventually, the Japanese also took control of Tientsin. We were furloughed in 1939. I took Florence and the girls to Toronto while I returned to Edinburgh. By now Britain was at war with Germany. I volunteered for the R.A.F., but they told me that at 37 I was too old to fly. The family joined me in Edinburgh in 1940. In August, all of us left once again for China. Florence worked as a nurse in Tientsin. I returned to Siaochang. Devastation was everywhere. The Japanese controlled the area, forcing the villagers to build roads. Town after town was destroyed in the fighting, and our hospital and church were filled with wounded. While we were not belligerents, the Japanese attitude to foreign nationals was becoming more negative. Missionaries were harassed.

In 1941 we were ordered to leave Siaochang. We learned later that it had been completely destroyed. Tientsin was also becoming unsafe. We learned that British nationals were likely to be interned. The mission board made arrangements for missionaries to leave. I sent Florence and the children to Toronto, but I decided to stay to see what I could do to help. I expected to follow shortly. I received a telegram in September telling me of the birth of our third daughter. I have not seen her.

In December of 1941, the Japanese attacked Pearl Harbor. Missionaries were ordered from their homes and required to move to the British neighborhood and to wear armbands displaying their nationality. Some of us applied for repatriation as part of an exchange of civilian nationals, but nothing came of it. In March of 1943, all enemy nationals were required to go to an internment camp in Shantung Province. The compound was a ruined American Presbyterian Mission station. Nothing worked. We had to organize a camp for 1,800 internees. Three hundred of them were children from a school for missionary children. I organized activities for the youth and became math and science teacher in the school we established. I tried to discourage Sunday games, but many of our inmates were business people who were indifferent to religious scruples.

Typhoid, malaria, dysentery, heat, and hunger have all taken their toll. As these months have progressed, I think all of us are slowly starving to death. I know my strength is not what it was.

Did I make a wrong decision in coming to China? No. I am confident that this is where God wanted me to be. Did I make a wrong decision in staying in China when my family left? Well, it was a wrong decision if my own well-being is the only consideration. But who knew for sure how any of this would turn out? I have been useful, and I believe that I have been faithful, and that gives me contentment. "... they that wait upon the Lord shall renew their strength, they shall mount up with wings like eagles, they shall run and not be weary, they shall walk and not faint."

Epilogue: Eric Liddell died on February 21, 1945, apparently from a brain tumor, while he was detained in a Japanese internment camp in Shantung Province, China. He was 43 years old.

11. When Christ Calls

Mark 8:31-38

"When Christ calls a man, he bids him come and die." I wrote those words back in the relative safety of 1937. Little did I realize then that those words were to be a prophecy of my own calling. Of course, at this moment, I am not dead yet, in this year of our Lord 1945, but I have been in prison for two years now, and in recent weeks, the Gestapo has been moving me around from prison to prison as though they have some definite plan for my ending. Just today, April 8, they brought me here to Flossenberg prison. They indicate that I will be tried tomorrow, though on what charge I am not sure. I don't know why they bother with a trial; they must have their minds made up already, to have kept me in prison so long.

I don't suppose you even know who I am. My name is Dietrich Bonhoeffer. I have been a Lutheran pastor and professor of Theology. I have written several books. Perhaps you have heard of the most popular one. It is called *The Cost of Discipleship*. It was published in 1937.

You might wonder, "What is a German pastor and theologian doing in a Nazi concentration camp?" My parents have wondered the same thing. When I was fourteen I informed my parents that I had decided that my life's work was to be in the field of religion. My father, a prominent psychiatrist in Berlin, was at first quite disappointed. But later, when the church was being persecuted by Hitler, my father wrote me a letter in which he said, "When you were a boy and I heard that you intended to enter the pastorate, I thought that this was not the way you should go, confining yourself to a corner of life ... Now, seeing the church in a crisis that I never thought would be possible, I see that what you have chosen was very right." Right, perhaps. But none of us knew then, that it would also be dangerous.

Permit me to share with you some of the things I have learned during these past years. I have been involved in a pilgrimage that has taken me from classroom to concentration camp, and I'm sure that you can understand that has had a profound effect on what I believe. At the very least, I have discovered that theology is not a list of propositions hammered out in a classroom or set down once and for all by church leaders of the past. It is something that develops in very concrete, this-worldly situations where one has to make hard decisions about his own destiny and that of others.

As I have spent a lot of time in prison, I have had considerable time to reflect on my own life and experiences, and I can see three rather definite periods in my own development which I would like to share with you.

I suppose that the first period of my life could be called theoretical: those halcyon days before the rise of Hitler. I was born in Bresslau, in 1906. While I was still a child, my family moved to Berlin, and it was by the University of Berlin that I was presented my theological degree in 1927. After pastoring a German colony in Barcelona, Spain, for a year and a half, I returned to Berlin and successfully presented a dissertation which won me a post as professor of Systematic Theology.

Before I took up my duties, however, I was invited to become a guest lecturer in theology, touring the United States. I made many friends in America and elsewhere in my travels, which led me to an awareness that Christ's Church is world-wide and not the special preserve of any nation. That awareness was to get me in trouble later. While I found much of the preaching in the American churches to be intellectually and spiritually empty, there was a sense of warmth and fellowship which our German churches were missing. Little did I realize then how much we in Germany were going to have to rely on our sister churches in America for support in a few short years.

I returned to Germany and took up my teaching duties at the University of Berlin. That was in 1931. I was also fully ordained as a pastor in the Lutheran Church in that year. In that year I also had a profound spiritual experience. Certainly, I had been intellectually prepared to teach theology, but it wasn't until 1931 that I discovered the Bible and prayer as personally rewarding elements in my spiritual development. I think it might be safe to say that in that year I became a Christian in the most personal sense of the word. I began to understand what it meant for the church really to be the body of Jesus Christ, the church as the person of Jesus Christ in the world. It became clear to me that the life of a servant of Jesus Christ must also belong to the church, and step by step, it became plain to me how far that must go.

In those days the Nazi menace was growing in Germany. In 1932, I commented that we should not be surprised if once again days should come for our church when the blood of martyrs would be demanded. In January, 1933, Adolf Hitler was installed as chancellor of Germany. Two days after Hitler came to power, I was presenting a radio message and I took the opportunity to warn the German people that the authority they were placing in the *fuhrer* would lead to idolatry. I was cut off the air before my message was completed.

I didn't realize it then, but I had embarked on the second phase of my Christian development, one that was to be marked by conflict with both government and the church. Hitler moved quickly to bend the church to his will. He developed the idea of "German Christians" as somehow unique and superior to others. He installed as head of the Protestant church a man who supported Nazi views. He passed laws barring anyone of Jewish origin, or married to a Jew, from holding any government office. He also excluded persons of Christian religion who held any office in the church.

Some of us who were opposed to these racist views organized a new structure which we called the Confessing Church. We issued a statement pointing out the errors we felt had been introduced into the church by the Nazi regime. In protest against these so-called "Aryan laws," I resigned my teaching post and accepted the pastorate of a German congregation in London, so that I could be free to tell the world that there was a church in Germany which did not go along with the Nazis.

In 1935, the Confessing Church called me back to Germany to organize a seminary for the training of pastors. We had some 35 pastors in training there. I wrote a book about our experiences which

I called *Life Together*. Sometimes a student, realizing the limitations of our small Confessing Church, would say that he would like to enter the larger State Church in order to have access to the larger pulpits, so that he might speak to more people about our concerns. On those occasions I would have to remind the student that "one act of obedience is better than one hundred sermons." Almost immediately after its formation, the seminary was outlawed as being seditious, but the Gestapo, involved with other things, didn't get around to closing us by force until 1937.

Though I was harassed by the Nazis, I continued to preach and lecture, and in 1937, I published what came to be my best-known book, *The Cost of Discipleship*. At this time I was particularly concerned about the Protestant emphasis on God's gracious forgiveness, which seemed to excuse a person from costly discipleship. I called this emphasis "cheap grace," and in the course of my book, I sought to show that being Christian and relying on God's grace doesn't excuse one from costly acts of loyalty. In fact, as I said at the beginning of my remarks, "When Christ calls a man, he bids him come and die."

In 1938, my brother-in-law introduced me to the resistance movement against the Nazis, what you might call "the underground." I had always been an absolute pacifist. In fact, I had confided to a friend a few years earlier that "when war comes I shall pray to Christ to give me the power not to take up arms." But I was beginning to see that it is not enough to follow Christ by preaching, teaching, and writing. Being a Christian must be translated into action and self-sacrifice. The Christian must not be shut away in sacramental piety, for we follow one who passed through this world as a living, dying, and risen Lord. I was beginning to see pacifism as an illegitimate escape.

In the midst of these thoughts I was invited on a lecture tour of the United States. Some of my brethren, concerned for my safety, and also wanting a representative of the Confessing Church to speak for them in America, urged me to go. I arrived in America in June of 1939, knowing that war was imminent. But my conscience was unsettled. Almost at once I wrote a letter to my American sponsors telling them that I had made a mistake in coming to America, that

I would have to live through this difficult period of our national history with the Christian people of Germany. I pointed out that I would have no right to participate in the reconstruction of Christian life in Germany after the war if I did not share the trials of this time with my people. My brethren in the Confessing Synod may have been right in urging me to go to America, but I was wrong in going. I felt that Christians in Germany would soon have to face the terrible alternative of either willing the defeat of their nation in order that Christian civilization might survive, or willing the victory of their nation and thereby destroying our civilization. I knew which of these alternatives I had to choose, but I could not make that choice in the security of another country, so I left America.

I returned to Germany and soon thereafter became active in the resistance. I saw Hitler as an anti-Christ who must be stopped. I became convinced that it is not only a Christian right, but also a Christian duty to oppose tyranny. In time, I was to work for the defeat, not only of Naziism, but even for the defeat of my own country, for I felt that only so could Germany be saved as a Christian country. Of all this, of course, the government knew nothing, but because of my previous statements, in 1940, the Gestapo stopped me from teaching, preaching, or publishing. No longer was I permitted the luxury of theoretical Christian opinion; I was being forced by circumstances to apply Christian principles in the sphere of life and death decisions about my own conduct.

The third phase of my Christian development began now as I became a political activist. My brother-in-law got me a job in the counter-intelligence office in Berlin, which, unknown to the government, had become the center of the revolt against Hitler. The Gestapo was apparently too preoccupied with other things to question my involvement in a government position. In that position I was permitted to travel on official business to certain neutral countries where I made contacts with the Allies, to determine if they would come to favorable terms with the resistance, if we could take over the government. The Allies offered us nothing. Nevertheless, we plotted to get rid of Hitler. What a change had occurred in my life and thought: from a Christian pacifist to a planner of assassination, and all out of loyalty to the same Lord. How circumstances control our Christian conduct! I appeal to you, therefore, not to judge others until you understand what they are up against!

In April, 1943, the Gestapo became aware that the counter-intelligence office was being used by the resistance. Though they did not know our plan, many of us were arrested. At first I was charged with treason, but lacking evidence, that charge was dropped, and I was simply held on a technicality of having spoken against the State. I lived daily with the thought that I would be charged and quickly released, but the Gestapo had other things in mind.

Prison life at best is a living death, cut off from those who make life meaningful. To be imprisoned without sentence is worse, because you are always telling yourself and others, "maybe tomorrow," "maybe next week," "maybe by Christmas," but nothing changes. By this time, nightly air raids had begun on Berlin, and the prisoners were in constant fear that we would be bombed and killed since we had no shelters. Frequently, I was able to minister to prisoners, some of them in their final hours. Therefore, prisoners and guards alike called me "Padre." I spent most of my time reading and writing, as I worked on several projects which were slipped out of prison, a few pages at a time, by friendly guards.

On July 20, 1944, some of the members of the resistance who were still free, managed to plant a bomb in Hitler's conference room. The bomb exploded, but Hitler survived, and personally directed the counter-revolutionary measures. Most of the conspirators were apprehended and executed. In October, the Gestapo found some records which firmly connected me with the resistance, and they subsequently moved me to a maximum security prison in Berlin, still without trial. I have not been able to contact my family since then. As Berlin has been threatened by the arrival of the Allies, I have been moved from one concentration camp to another, while the Gestapo tries to decide what to do with me. In spite of what I have been through, I have never regretted my decision to return to Germany in 1939. I am sure of God's hand and guidance, and I am thankful and glad to go the way in which I have been led.

As I said previously, these past two years have had considerable impact on my thinking. I have discovered what I call a "Christian worldliness." By that I mean that we must not think that God and the Christian faith are concerned only with the ultimate outcome of things in some future eternity. We have responsibility for things in the present moment, and we must take action. To labor for civil rights, to engage in political struggle on behalf of the disadvantaged, to do battle with ignorance, poverty, and disease: these are things that cannot be dismissed as secular and unspiritual. In fact, every attempt to make people more truly human is a Christian act, whether the name of Christ is mentioned specifically or not. In Christ, God and the world have been inseparably joined. Therefore, we cannot think of Christianity as being concerned only with the next world; Christ is Lord of all creation.

Not only have I discovered a "Christian worldliness," but a "religionless Christianity." In some ways religion is the enemy of Christianity. Religion is individualistic: it can make one so concerned for his own soul that he abandons his neighbors in need. Religion is metaphysical and often looks to another world when it should be dealing with this one. Religion tends to be provincial and to concentrate on smaller and smaller segments of life which it calls "religious," when its view should encompass all of life. Moreover, religion tends to appeal to God to intervene in the course of things so that consequences won't follow actions, which is irresponsible. What matters in the church, then, is not the growth of religion, but the development of the body of Christ. Jesus is supremely "the man for others," and the church is only the church when it exists for humanity. Only a servant church can earn the right to speak with authority and power in our secular age.

And now my pilgrimage has brought me here to Flossenburg concentration camp. Perhaps you feel I am here for political activity; I believe I am here as a servant of Jesus Christ in a difficult time. They have just called my name. I know what that means. Take to heart what I have said. A Christian has no other choice as a free moral agent, than to act, to suffer, and if need be, to die. Suffering is the badge of true discipleship. When Christ calls *you,* may *you* find the strength to do what is required.

Epilogue: Dietrich Bonhoeffer was hanged by the Nazis at Flossenburg Prison on April 9, 1945, one month before World War II ended in Germany.

12. Through Gates Of Splendor

Matthew 16:21-28

The Aucas have been on my heart since the first time I heard about them at a missionary conference while I was still in college. They have always been a fierce people. They killed Spanish conquistadors in the sixteenth century and speared a Jesuit priest, the first missionary trying to contact them, in 1667. They were left alone for 200 years. In the nineteenth century, rubber hunters raided their villages, carted off able-bodied young men to be slaves, and killed others to prevent reprisal. There could have been cooperation, but the conduct of white people ended that. It is no wonder that they have stayed aloof and have avoided contact with white people. Oil explorers here in Ecuador had to contend with them in the 1940s, and occasionally lost a worker to their attacks. It is assumed that there are 500 to 1,000 of them living in small settlements in the jungle around us. And to think that we have been privileged to contact them, and that we will meet a group of them for the first time this very day! All of us are excited. I can hardly wait! Let me tell you how it came to pass that we are here at this moment.

My name is Jim Elliot. I was born in Portland, Oregon, in 1927. I was raised in a Christian home, and I have been an enthusiastic Christian all my life. I attended Wheaton College, an evangelical college in Illinois. In my sophomore year, I felt the call to be a missionary to Latin America. I majored in Greek in preparation for translating the New Testament into other languages, and I studied Spanish informally. I felt convinced that God was calling me to work among the unreached Indians of South America. I met another Wheaton student, Elizabeth Howard, while I was a sophomore, and, though we came to love one another, I felt that it was essential that I go to the mission field, at least initially, as a single person.

A friend of mine, Pete Fleming, had just gotten his M.A. in Literature from the University of Washington. People thought he would be a teacher, but he, too, felt called to go to Ecuador, so the two of us teamed up, were commissioned by a Mission Board, and set sail from San Pedro, California, in February, 1952.

Before leaving the ship at Guayaquil, we sang that hymn: "Faith of our fathers, holy faith, we will be true to thee till death." That was an accurate statement of our own conviction. We flew to Quito, Ecuador, where we spent six months in an intensive study of Spanish.

Following our language training, we boarded a rickety bus that took us and our gear to the interior station of Shell Mera, an abandoned oil company town that served as the headquarters of the Missionary Aviation Fellowship. There we met Dr. Tidmarsh, who was to escort us to Shandia, a mission outpost among the Quichua Indians where Dr. Tidmarsh had served, but which he had had to abandon because of his wife's health. There was no airstrip at Shandia, so when we walked into their village, we were immediately surrounded by these gentle people who lived between the headhunting Jivaros to the south, fierce Aucas to the northeast, and the rising white people's world to the west. We had come to share God's word, but we would first have to live among them to gain their trust. Pete and I slowly became familiar with their language. Their language was not written, so we were constantly writing what we heard in little notebooks. The Indians asked Dr. Tidmarsh if we did anything else. As we learned more of the language, the Indians included us in more of their activities. Dr. Tidmarsh eventually returned to his home and left us in charge of the station. With medical books, penicillin, and prayer, we were often called on to help the sick in conjunction with the rituals of the witch doctor. We reopened the school room and tried to educate the youngsters so that one day they could bring the message of Christ to their people. We could see that we would always be outsiders.

In September, 1953, Ed McCully, one of my classmates at Wheaton, arrived with his wife and child to work with us at Shandia. Ed had taken a course in missionary medicine following graduation from college, and his knowledge would be a tremendous help. Pete and I built a house for the McCullys, and then, in a flood, it and all the other buildings were washed away. Five hundred hand-planed boards, each representing a day's work, were also swept away, along with 300 feet of the airstrip we had been clearing. We did what we had to do — rebuild. At the same time, the McCullys were learning the language, treating the sick, and keeping the station going.

Our life-line with the outside world was Nate Saint, a pilot with the Missionary Aviation Fellowship, who with his wife Marj was stationed at Shell Mera, where they had built a mission facility and hangar. Marj monitored the radio for contacts with MAF planes and with outlying mission stations. Before the arrival of the Saints, missionaries might have to trek through the jungle for eight days to get simple supplies. Now, with an airstrip and short-wave radio, things could be brought in by plane in forty minutes. It made our work more efficient, healthier, and safer. Nate had developed a way to lower a bucket on a line so that people on the ground in areas where there was no airstrip could put things in or take things out, including the use of a field telephone, while the plane circled.

Not too far away from us by plane was another couple working among the Jivaros. Roger Youderian, his wife Barbara, and their two children were working at Macuma, another jungle outpost. They, too, had studied missionary medicine and came to Ecuador in 1953. They have studied the Jivaro language and developed a method of teaching the Jivaros to read and write in their own language. It is a difficult place to work, because the Jivaros live by revenge. Children are taught early the names of people they must hate and are encouraged to take reprisal against any relative of those they hate. The love taught by Jesus is foreign to their way of thinking.

Roger has wanted to go deeper into the jungle and work where no missionary has been. He feels a great urgency to save souls. In 1954 Roger moved his work to a remote abandoned airstrip at Wambuni, where he could be nearer an unreached tribe, the Atshuaras, who are cousins, but deadly enemies, of the Jivaros. Because of some medical successes he was invited to their village and was, in fact, able to save many Indians from death when a roving band of soldiers inadvertently brought influenza into their village.

89

I went back to the States in 1953 to marry Elizabeth and to bring her with me to Ecuador. In November of that year we opened a station at Puyupungu to teach Indian children. In 1954 Pete returned to the States to marry his fiancee, Olive, and in the fall of 1955 they came to relieve us at Puyupungu so we could return to Shandia. We were now deployed so that we could make contact with the elusive Aucas.

In October of 1955, Ed McCully, another MAF pilot, and I were looking at a map, planning how we might contact the Aucas. We knew that we needed to keep our plans secret from the Indians among whom we were working and from anyone who might be listening to our radio messages, because at first contact competitive commercial groups would quickly follow up on any contact we might make. We referred to the Aucas simply as the "neighbors." Ed and Nate had discovered what looked like an Auca settlement just fifteen minutes by plane from where the McCullys were stationed. We decided to make gift drops using the spiraling cable Nate had developed. At the same time I went to interview an Auca woman who had come out of the jungle and to learn phrases of their language.

The first gift drop on October 6, 1955, consisted of a tea kettle, rock salt, buttons, and streamers. It was dropped on a sandbar near a large communal house by means of a release mechanism in a bucket. No one was in sight, but a week later, when a machete was dropped, four men came out and ran for the machete. Subsequently Nate hooked up a loudspeaker on the plane so that as we dropped gifts, I would call out in their language, "I like you. I am your friend," or "We have come to pay a visit." The Indians would now wave at us. They showed no sign of hostility or fear. We continued to make drops and speak on the loudspeakers. The Indians learned to take things out of the bucket as we circled, and eventually, they began to put gifts in the bucket for us: feathered head-bands, live birds, food. I was anxious to go in. I prayed, "God, send me soon." I felt the Aucas were saying, "Come down." The three of us felt we needed more help, so we invited Roger Youderian and Pete Fleming to join us, which they did.

Now we had to look for a place to land. We named the village that had received the gifts "Terminal City." As we continued to drop gifts, we noticed that one of the huts had a model airplane on its roof, a sign to us of goodwill.

We decided to make January 3, 1956, the date of our ground contact. We decided we would wear the headdresses they had provided so they would recognize us, that we would carry small airplanes, that we would carry small gifts wrapped as previous ones had been, that we would shout, "I like you," in their language. We also decided that we would have handguns available to frighten off Indians if they should happen to attack us. We also knew that the first shot fired would be the end of our mission. We tested several sandbars as possible landing sites, and chose one we named "Palm Beach." We planned to make several trips with supplies and building materials all in the same day. We would plan for a five-day stay, but have supplies for twelve days in case of siege or flood. We included air mattresses for floating downstream, should that become necessary. We continued to make gift drops, including pictures of ourselves, and the Indians continued to put gifts in the bucket: a parrot, a woven basket, a distaff for spinning cotton yarn, fruit, a squirrel, some pottery.

All of us, including our wives, felt that God's leading was unmistakable, but we were also realistic about the dangers. Our wives considered among themselves what they would do if we were killed. Each of us felt we had made a personal transaction with God, and that we were at God's disposal. We had heard Christ's call to go into all the world with the Good News of God's love, and the issue of personal safety was irrelevant. Nate Saint expressed the feeling of all of us when he wrote "... we feel that it is pleasing to God that we should interest ourselves in making an opening into the Auca prison for Christ."

Last Monday we all gathered with our families and our supplies at the McCullys' in Arajuno. On Tuesday morning we had breakfast together, prayed, sang a hymn, loaded the plane, and Nate took off with Ed. They had a safe landing on the beach, unloaded the plane, and Ed stayed at Palm Beach with the supplies. Next Nate flew in with Roger and me and more supplies. We set up a platform in a tree as a place to stay. On his way back to Arajuno, Nate flew over the village and broadcast in their language, "Come tomorrow to the Curaray River." The three of us who were staying at Palm Beach would stand on the beach and call out toward the trees, using phrases in the Auca language. On Thursday the jungle was still quiet, but we felt we were being watched. The village itself we determined to be about a day's walk through the jungle from where we were. Nate was flying in each day with supplies, staying for the day, and flying out in the evening with letters, messages, and films.

On Friday an Auca man and two women appeared from the jungle as we were bombarding the jungle with words. They jabbered among themselves and to us, with no comprehension that we couldn't understand them. We took pictures, gave gifts, showed them magazines. They seemed unafraid. We called the man George. He showed interest in the plane and a willingness to fly, so Pete flew him over the village. He waved and yelled to those below. When the plane returned, George jumped out clapping his hands in glee. We offered thanks to God.

We served them lemonade and hamburgers with mustard, which they evidently enjoyed. We tried to get George to invite us to his village, but he seemed reluctant. Early Saturday morning they disappeared into the jungle. All yesterday we waited for others to arrive with an invitation to their village. Nate flew over the village broadcasting, "Come, come, come." He could see George back in the village.

This morning Pete flew over the village, and he noticed that some of the men were on the trail to the beach. He flew back and announced, "This is it, guys. They're on the way." We radioed Marj, told her of the expected arrival, and asked that she and the others pray for us. We expect the Aucas to arrive about 4:00 this afternoon. All five of us are here now, and we're pretty excited. Whatever comes of this, we believe that God will use us to open the door to these people, to make it possible for them to hear about the love of God, to experience through us the salvation that is possible through faith in our Lord Jesus Christ. Though what we are doing is dangerous, we are grateful to be a part of it. Anyway, we all feel that that person is no fool who gives up what he cannot keep to attain what he cannot lose. May God be glorified and people saved by what we will be doing today.

Epilogue: There was no further message from the five young missionaries. At the first meeting with the larger group of Aucas, the Indians became frightened, attacked the missionaries, killed them, destroyed the plane, and returned to their village. Soldiers found and buried the bodies. A year later Elizabeth Elliot, her five-year-old daughter, and Nate Saint's sister went to live among the Aucas and were accepted by them. The Indians said that it had been a mistake to kill the missionaries. Nevertheless, their deaths opened the door for the Aucas to receive the message of God's love.